Call Me By Your Name:

How a Little Film Touched So Many Lives

Written by Devoted Fans From All Over the World

D0815889

Compiled and Edited by Barb Mirell

ISBN: 9780998762562 - paperback

 Published by Liberty Bell Publishers

325 Chestnut Street Suite 800

Philadelphia, PA 19106

www.libertybellpublishers.com

ACKNOWLEDGEMENTS

This book is dedicated to novelist André Aciman, director Luca Guadagnino, screenwriter James Ivory, actors Armie Hammer, Timothée Chalamet, Michael Stuhlbarg, Amira Casar, Esther Garrel, Victoire Du Bois, Vanda Capriolo, and Antonio Rimoldi, editor Walter Fasano, cinematographer Sayombhu Mukdeeprom, composer Sufjan Stevens, the producers, and everyone involved in the making *of Call Me By Your Name.*

Thank you for changing our lives!

A Note From the Editor

I remember seeing ads for *Call Me By Your Name* last year. *"A life changing film – Indie Wire"* splashed across the screen. I scoffed. How could a movie do that? But it was no exaggeration as I found out later when I saw the movie for myself.

The story of star-crossed lovers Oliver and Elio in Northern Italy was an emotional, cinematic masterpiece. As the film ended, there were lots of sniffles and people crying in the audience. I left the theater in a daze, misty-eyed, with a lump in my throat. Wow, what a great movie!

But what seemed at first to be a simple, bittersweet love story was in fact a multi-layered and profound experience. And I definitely was not prepared for the aftermath. I could not get that damn film out of my head. It haunted me for days. It was the last thing I thought about before I fell asleep and the first thing when I woke up. That is, if I could fall asleep.

I had the worst insomnia of my life as I found myself replaying scenes in my head. If this had happened twenty years ago, it might have been different. However, with my computer tablet bedside, I could not resist re-watching scenes that were uploaded. There were dozens of montages and music videos made by devotees and I couldn't resist playing them over and over.

Sufjan Steven's songs were earworms that repeated in my head (*Is it a video? Is it a video?*) throughout the day. I had trouble concentrating at work. And more than anything, I felt melancholic and had a terrible headache that simply would not go away.

Why was I so preoccupied with this movie? I went online to find out more about the film and was astonished to see there were hundreds of postings from people who were also haunted. They called it the "*Call Me By Your Name Syndrome*" and many had similar physical and mental reactions:

I became overwhelmed with powerful emotions days later.

This story will not leave my mind ... I have trouble thinking of anything else.

I am a wreck. I've actually lost weight.

I want to watch the movie over and over.

It is affecting my work life.

People revealed intimate details about their lives, there was fan fiction involving Elio and Oliver, even a support group for people who literally thought they were going crazy.

This film did something to me; I feel paralyzed.

I have a knot in my stomach ... and have difficulty concentrating on anything else ...

It was also interesting to note that even though the movie was upsetting, like masochists we watched it repeatedly - some people dozens of times. It seemed that everyone read the original book by André Aciman and/or listened to the audiobook, narrated by Armie Hammer. Why were we torturing ourselves?

What can account for this obsession? Reading the posts, I found that this multi-layered film brought back a lot of repressed memories and had some people re-evaluating their lives. There were many aspects that affected these viewers, including:

People who grew up in dysfunctional families: The very open and loving Perlman family were physically and verbally affectionate. They hugged each other while passing in the hallways and used terms of endearment toward each other. They were supportive of their son's same sex romance, which especially struck gay men who were ostracized by their families or had to hide their sexual preferences.

Oh, how my life would have been different if I had a family like this!

People regretting not telling someone they loved them. A recurrent theme throughout the movie is - "Is it better to speak or to die?" First spoken by Elio's mother as she reads him a French tale involving a knight who loves a princess but cannot tell her, the phrase is repeated throughout. This "road not taken" view really seemed to strike a nerve with a lot of people. It takes courage to risk unrequited love. Many pondered how their lives would have turned out if they would have said something.

I keep thinking about someone in college that I never had the nerve to talk to ...

It left me quite depressed ... thinking about what ifs.

Nostalgically remembering the infatuation and giddiness of falling in love. Memories of youth and yearning for those simple times again. Even those who were in happy relationships longed for those days when everything was new and exciting.

It made me question what love really is.

Lonely people who had never experienced love or were not currently in a relationship. *Call Me By Your Name* is an extremely romantic and sensuous film. So realistic were the love scenes, that many of those posting simply could not accept that Chalamet and Hammer were straight actors and not lovers in real life. The kissing and gentle caresses showed a tenderness between the on-screen lovers that is indeed rare.

This film rekindled my desire to find love again after so many years.

People remembering the devastation of having their hearts broken. To many, Professor Perlman's masterful monologue when consoling his heartbroken son was the heart of the film. "Our hearts and our bodies are given to us only once. And before you know it, your heart is worn out, and, as for your body, there comes a point when no one looks at it, much less wants to come near it. Right now, there's sorrow, pain. Don't kill it and with it the joy you've felt." This scene was the one that affected most people.

I realized that I never really got over my first heartbreak.

I have never been much of a crier. I didn't even cry when either of my parents died. And as I re-watched the film over the next week, I again would just get choked up and a bit misty.

But one day, I noticed someone uploaded the very end of the film. As the credits roll, we watch a closeup of Timothée Chalamet's face as tears streamed down. I couldn't hold it in any longer.

Memories of lovers long ago, the times that I was too afraid to speak, the loneliness I felt since the death of my sweetheart washed over me. I sobbed uncontrollably, and it felt so good to let it all out. The next morning I woke up and my headache was gone.

When I discovered the *Call Me by Your Name Global Facebook Page*, I felt like I had found a new family. They referred to each other as "peaches". People from all over the world: men and women, from teenagers to seniors, all religions and races, gay, straight and bisexual: all connected by this one film and how it affected them.

The stories that people shared were moving. We discussed interpretations and symbolism throughout the book and movie. Members helped each other when they were going through rough times. True friendships were formed as people talked via Skype, private messaged, texted each other, and met each other in person.

I traveled to New York to meet other "peaches" and hear André Aciman speak about the book and his writing. Although we had just met, it was like a reunion of old friends.

I put the word out asking people to tell me how *Call Me By Your Name* has affected them. Here are their stories.

--Barb Mirell

From Heather Damitz –

Administrator of the Call Me By Your Name Global Facebook Group

"Now we shan't never be parted. It's finished." How I loved that line at the end of *Maurice*, James Ivory's film adaptation of E.M. Forster's novel. At the end of *Call Me By Your Name*, I knew that Oliver would not be saying a version of that to Elio, I braced myself for the final scene, but was eviscerated nonetheless. The pain of first heartbreak is a universal language, one we all speak, and one that unites us. *Call Me By Your Name* is unique in its ability to find those memories, those possibilities, or missed opportunities for love and have them be as fresh as the day they were happening.

After seeing the film, reading the book or a version of the two, many people find themselves looking for an outlet to talk about their feelings, share experiences, or simply keep being part of the experience. Call Me By Your Name Global was formed to be an inclusive group for members from all over the world to express themselves and their love for all things CMBYN-related.

The story of Elio and Oliver is first owed to the author of *Call Me By Your Name*, Andre Aciman, without whom these characters would not exist. Luca Guadagnino, whose direction brought the story to life on screen. Screenplay writer James Ivory, who adopted the work fluidly. Timothée Chalamet, Armie Hammer, and the entire cast of the film who brought the characters to life for us, the audience.

Call Me By Your Name Global and the Peach family would not exist without the tireless efforts of co-founder Ed Hernandez and Rebecca Elliot. They have made great efforts to maintain a loving, warm environment in which members can express themselves. Thanks also goes out to our newest team member Rose J Mort. CMBYN Global wishes to also thank CDT and MGD for their contributions. And to all the members who make this group a family, thank you.

From Frank Drake –

Administrator of Call Me By Your Name Fan Support Group on Twitter (@CMBYNFANSUPPORT)

Many of the greatest films of all time have never won Academy Awards. Many of the best films were never even nominated for Oscars. *Call Me By Your Name* was nominated for 4 Academy Awards and won the Oscar for Best Adapted Screenplay by James Ivory.

We have to remember that critiques, reviews and awards are all subjective. It is one person or a group of eligible voters' consensus on what is the "best" for that year. The film is the art. The film will stand the test of time. Many films find their audience well after their run in theaters. Sometimes, it takes years for this to happen. Many movies do not do well at the box office and fade from theaters.

The CMBYN fandom is huge, it's massive and it is global. Soon after I first saw *Call Me By Your Name* in December 2017, I felt a need to discuss the film and to seek out others to see how they felt about the movie. I created a *Call Me By Your Name Fan Support Group* on Twitter.

Much to my surprise, I was greeted enthusiastically by others who loved the film, felt devastated by it, and simply needed to talk about the movie. Fans have discussed all aspects of the movie from its beautiful love story, exceptional performances, the exquisite Italian countryside to the outstanding soundtrack that enhances the film.

Another overwhelming aspect in creating this support group is how global an audience that CMBYN has impacted. I have followers from all over the world. Tom Pe @AlwaysWouldBe from New York is a huge fan of the film having seen it over 85 times in the movie theater. AG de la Cruz @cryospherical from Bangkok is another supporter of *Call Me By Your Name* and the film has affected him deeply.

These are just two of hundreds of followers who have been affected by *Call Me By Your Name*. We have all formed a genuine bond and friendship from our love of this beautiful work of art.

This Academy Award-winning cinematic masterpiece is breathtaking. The film is changing lives. It has changed my life. No film has impacted my life like this since Steven Soderbergh's *Sex, Lies and Videotape* in 1989.

The relationship that develops between Elio and Oliver is a reminder to all of us about our first love. The film has resonated deeply amongst its most loyal supporters. It is beautiful. It is devastating. It is hopeful. It is heartbreaking. It made me realize that life is short, and every single day needs to be lived to the fullest.

The film has helped me to make the decision to come out to live my life as a gay man. I think I had been living in a state of limbo for so long that I didn't feel anything. *Call Me By Your Name* made me feel again. It has made me want to live life again. It has made me want to explore all the things I have been afraid to do in life for so long. As I continue on my journey, I will be making a trip to Italy to visit as many CMBYN filming locations as I can on my "Eat, Gay, Love Tour".

I know that many of us in the *Call Me By Your Name* fandom have been disappointed with the award season this year. I am generally a very pessimistic person, but I'm choosing optimism. Look at everything this small independent film has achieved from start to finish.

André Aciman wrote this magnificent love story in 2007 and it took 10 years for this masterful work of art to make it to the big screen. The film earned four Academy Award nominations for Best Picture, Best Adapted Screenplay for James Ivory (the oldest nominee and now winner in this category), Best Original Song *Mystery of Love* by Sufjan Stevens and Best Actor for Timothée Chalamet (the youngest nominee to be nominated in this category in 80 years). The film has gone on to be a worldwide success and global phenomenon.

As with any piece of art, it is timeless and will be appreciated in the years and decades to come. But the CMBYN fandom was here from the beginning. We identified with Elio and Oliver. We hoped to become like The Perlman's. We lost ourselves in the film's spectacular cinematography, set design, costumes and music soundtrack. We fell in love with "Olio" while exploring their love for one another that evolved naturally between two human beings. No labels, just natural love. We felt their pain upon their separation. (A heartbreaking, devastating pain that has lasted months since I saw the film, much like life.) But in all the heartbreak, we experienced love and for that we won't cry because it's over, but smile because it happened.

"We had found the stars, you and I. And this is given once only."

André Aciman, Call Me by Your Name

Thoughts From Fans:

Why CMBYN means so much to me: I'm not looking for sympathy just telling my story in the hope that it may help someone else. Here it goes...Oddly enough my first love was one of my closest childhood friends. His family moved about an hour away, so I didn't see him as much during our high school years but then perhaps by fate we both attended the same College. He was extremely intelligent, spoke six languages fluently, was a voracious reader, and could talk on any subject.

As gay teens in the 80's we were both very isolated but our saving grace was we confided everything to each other. We shared our innermost thoughts and desires to the point where he would know what I was thinking before I did and vice versa. In adolescence we experimented a little, but the romance really began in College. We had five amazing years together as a couple, but because our parents were best friends and not at all tolerant we had to keep it a secret.

I have great memories of our vacations and breaks from school spent together. He was a constant in my life for eighteen years that I thought would always be there for me. We almost never fought, but then abruptly without any explanation he broke off our relationship.

After a cooling-off period, we resumed contact but as time went on we talked less frequently. We both attended a wedding five years after our break up and had a blast dancing and drinking that night. We were both feeling no pain after the festivities and we slept together like old times. Nothing happened although I had the feeling he sort of wanted something to happen, but I wrote if off to the alcohol.

Shortly after that I heard he was having an addiction problem. I reached out to him multiple times, but he never would talk about it. I saw him briefly a few more times over the next decade.

I will never forget the call I got that he took his life. Strangely enough, about the exact time of his death I had thoughts of him that came rushing into my consciousness which I now interpret as his spirit saying good bye to me.

I went to the funeral and I've never felt so sick at heart in all my life. His mother told me that when they cleaned out his place they found a letter from me written many years before that was tattered and careworn, like he had read it a million times and held on to it until it was nearly illegible. I was completely crushed because I didn't know he still had those feelings for me. I remember all that we shared down to the most minute details. I wish he could have lived to see the strides the LGBT community has made. I think he would love Call Me By Your Name as I do.

Timothy Schraw
Cincinnati, OH
USA

I have never been an emotive person. It takes a long time and a lot of trust for me show how I am really feeling. Because of this, I have often been called "cold", "heartless" and even asexual. I can't count the number of times I've been told "you should smile more". Some don't understand that this lack of showing emotions doesn't mean I don't have any.

I can't recall a time when I have cried during a film. Until *Call Me by Your Name*. I cried once during the theater showing, which was during the Dad's speech, but who didn't? Repeated viewings of this movie made me cry multiple times throughout, which was highly unlikely for me to do.

What is it about this film and book that turned an emotionally repressed person into a puddle of tears? I can't say for certain. Maybe it's the beauty of the location. Italy is stunning on its own merit. Is it the idea of the perfect summer? Sun, books, music, and fresh fruit. Who wouldn't fall in love with that? Or could it be that I am Elio? I am him. I didn't notice so much while watching the film. But reading the book in which we get more of the depth Elio's thoughts, I discovered that he is me. I've had all his thoughts myself. Historically I've acted like him when attracted to someone. I'm aloof, I act nonchalant, I shun away from phys-ical interaction with said person. I do all this in hopes that they will see through it. That they will read my mind and reach out to me first. But that never happens. They always find someone else to love, marry and start a happy life …without me.

I suppose, these actions on my part are the reason I'm 36 years old and without a husband. I long ago made the life decision to not have children. For various reasons, I know (and always knew) that motherhood was not for me. However, I have not intentionally make the decision to be with-out a companion, a partner, a lover.

I also did not make the decision to be attracted to both men and women. That's something that just happened to me and you can't choose who you are attracted to. One would think that being flexible about gender would increase the chance of finding love. But it has not happened for me. I guess it could happen to me, but I'm not expecting it. For me, at this moment, love is like *Call Me by Your Name*: beautiful, magical, am-biguous and completely fictional.

Terri
State College, PA
USA

I am absolutely in love with this film. Everything about it was so well done. I saw the movie before I read the book. I am a crier. I cry when I watch beautiful movies or emotional ones. This did it for me! The emo-tions, how raw the characters were, how they both opened up. But it came with a price: heartbreak for both of them; they were both con-flicted. Do they take a chance on love, knowing the end result? Elio was more open then Oliver. I felt like that in my life.

I was in love once. He was younger. We were a lot alike. He knew me better then I knew myself. The only issue was he was gay. I told him he was. People didn't like that we were friends. We fought and cut ties for a very long time. We speak now. We both saw the movie and I told him he was my first love. He never knew that and told me he didn't know what to say. I told him "Don't say anything." I just had to tell him.

I have another gay best friend. We went to see *Call Me by Your Name* together and the movie reminded him of his ex-boyfriend. Like the father said in the movie, there is pain and sorrow. That speech made me cry so much. I felt like Elio and Oliver. Loving someone and losing them.

But you have the memories, no matter if they are alive or not. I lost my best friend who was more like a sister, in a car accident over the Christmas holiday. I have my memories of her. There is pain there. I lost my grandmother last year. We have our memories. We all go through things in life that make us stronger, which is how we overcome the next hurdle we have to face.

Thank you, Luca, for making this film. Thank you Armie and thank you Timothée for making these characters come alive on screen. And for all of us that came away with a little piece of it that will be with us for the rest of our lives.

Elisheva Rosenfeld
Monsey, NY
USA

I was completely sucked into this vintage Italian romance. I couldn't believe how moved I was by this film. For the first time, a movie made me fall in love, cry and feel a great sense of loss out of empathy for the characters.

It surprised me because it also made me realize how emotionally dead I was. I'd gotten into this habit of ignoring all my emotions, because I found it easier to feel nothing. But the movie reminded me that if you stifle the feeling of pain, you also stifle happiness and joy because they only really exist together. It made me feel something again and I've decided I'd rather feel joy and love, just to have even a morsel of what the characters had, even if it means the risk of feeling pain.

Anonymous
London
UK

A very unexpected outcome of my *Call Me by Your Name* addiction happened when I joined the *Call Me By Your Name Global Facebook Page*. We discuss every aspect of the film and all topics, no matter how trivial. I got quite an education. For example, we talked about the art in Elio's bedroom. The 1981 Roland Garros poster? I didn't know that was French Open tennis tournament. The photo of Robert Mapplethorpe? I wanted to find out more.

Discussions of the Sufjan Stevens' *Visions of Gideon* led me to look up the story of the biblical Gideon and parallels with Elio. The classical music soundtrack introduced me to John Adams and Ryuichi Sakamoto and then I listened to more of their pieces.

Similarities with earlier Merchant/Ivory, Eric Rohmer and Bernardo Bertolucci films made me want to re-watch movies I hadn't seen in years.

Professor Perlman's discussion of the Greek sculptor Praxiteles had me Googling him and learning about other similar artists.

Oliver's research on the philosopher Heraclitus made me want to read *The Cosmic Fragments* that was shown.

Every time I watch *Call Me By Your Name*, I discover something that piques my curiosity and that has never happened with any other film. I do not have much formal education, but I love learning new things!

Anonymous

Call Me by Your Name changed my life in so many ways. I believe in my dreams again and I believe in film making again.

Armie, you are my inspiration and motivation for my own screenplay and it's going great. Let me tell you a little bit about myself. My family works in the film business. My dad was producing some in Germany and Europe and all of my cousins are actors in Germany or somewhere else in this world. I don't know, and I don't care. I'm an only child and the black sheep of the family. Being gay is no go for them.

My mom never had a problem with that and she always supported me. Unfortunately, she died in a car accident over 15 years ago. From that day on, I was no longer welcome in my family.

So I moved on with my life, went to Los Angeles and to acting school. I did a few little things, but nothing big.

Came back to Germany a couple of years ago for private reasons. Since then, I work for a radio station here in Cologne.

I love it because I love music, but it's not enough.

After I watched *Call Me by Your Name* the first time, I knew that is the direction I want to go. I want to tell stories and it's about time that we tell our stories to the world.

Like I said before, Luca you did an amazing job. You showed people there's nothing wrong with being gay or bisexual.

Armie, you're my number one inspiration and motivation. I love your work and I hope that we can work together sooner or later.

Timothée, you've got a great future ahead of you. Keep going, my man.

Amira, in the movie you reminded me to my own mom. You're a great actress.

Michael, I wish I would have had a father like you played in the movie. It always brings me to tears. Excellent performance.

You all together are such an amazing team and I hope you work on a sequel. I also would love to work with you sooner or later. I have to go my own way.

I changed my last name and I don't want to have anything to do with my family anymore.

To you guys, I thank you and I love you. Have fun and keep it peachy.

Tom Swearington
Cologne, Germany
and
Los Angeles, CA

I can relate to *Call Me by Your Name* because of my experience in high school. There was this guy named Johnny in our circle of friends who was very handsome, and a lot of girls wanted to go out with him. He was two years older than me and I had a crush on him since I first met him.

During our junior year in high school, things started to change. He talked to me more and spent more time hanging out with our group of friends. As our junior year progressed, he and I spent time together. During the second semester of our junior year, my feelings for him got stronger. By the same token, he would stop by my class and wait for me. He would walk with me and carry my books, whether I stopped by my locker or went directly to my next class. In the morning, he would stop by my house, so we could walk to school together. He also asked me to wait for him until he finished his practice (he was on the track and field team).

Most of our girlfriends would ask me to set up a date with him, knowing that he and I were close. I did oblige, so they would not think of anything else. They started questioning me about my relationship with him. I told them that we were just friends. At night he would either call me when my parents were asleep or stop by my house just to hang around.

There was this instance that I will never forget and every time I remember it, gives me a good feeling. This happened in our senior year in high school.

One day, our group of friends decided to ditch school for the day. Since my parents weren't home and wouldn't be home until after 6 p.m., I told everyone that we could hang out at my house until after school. So we all did. As high school kids normally do, we played cards and drank some beers. Johnny and the rest of our friends started drinking. I didn't fear that anyone would get too drunk and start making trouble. Time went by and some of our friends started getting drunk. Johnny didn't, but he did ask me if he could take a cold shower to sober up. As he was getting ready to jump in the shower, he called me and told me to join him. I said no because I knew what was going to happen, but he insisted. As I jumped in the shower with him, I turned my back, so he wouldn't see my hard-on. He then asked me to scrub his back ... and I said to myself... FUCK!!! I quickly gave him a back rub and jumped out of the shower. I was hoping that none of our friends would see me coming out of the bathroom.

During our senior year, our friendship got stronger. We spent more time together and hung out - just the two of us. But good things come to an end. We would always write in our yearbook ... blah blah blah and keep in touch. But what he wrote was something different ... "I enjoy our friendship and time together"

After high school graduation, I stayed home and went to a community college. He in turn moved out and lived with his siblings in another city. A few years down the road, I moved on and so did he. I heard that he was back living with his parents. I got a hold of him and invited him for a drink. We went out and had a good time, but I needed to tell him how I felt about him during our high school year. I couldn't get the courage until I was close to his place. I couldn't say whether he was surprised or mad or what because after that night, I tried to contact him to no avail. I saw him on Facebook and sent a friend request, but he never responded.

That's why this movie meant so much to me. I could feel how Elio felt when he was crushing on Oliver. This movie means so much to me, brings back good feelings and not so good feelings. Johnny was a part of my life and wherever he is, maybe our paths will cross again.

Julian Garcia
Corona, CA
USA

I was so blown away by *Call Me By Your Name*, that I watched nearly every YouTube fan video that was made. And there were hundreds! Most had music from contemporary artists. As one who listens to mostly oldies, I was blown away. I don't listen to the radio as I think most contemporary music is crap, so it was a revelation discovering both famous and obscure singers Lana Del Rey, Greg Laswell, Sherrie Lea, Dead Man's Bones, Troye Sivan, The Irrepressibles, and Vassilikos.

It really made realize that there is still good music being made today!

Anonymous

For me, what the film did was help give me a lot of strength back to move forward with my life.

I have been blessed with the joy of so many of those emotions which are celebrated in this film. I paid the price, however, for that joy. For every piece of joy that I'd experienced, there was also equal intensity of betrayal and abandonment, leading to the inescapable assumption that maybe all of my instincts had been wrong in the first place.

Fortunately, I sought answers, and was able to put all of my questions at

 least reasonably to rest. That didn't erase the pain, however. The imprint of all of that bad, very menacingly overshadowing the good.

This film, from start to finish, reinforces the notion to not let the bad wipe out the surviving truth of those wonderful life-sustaining emotions that I'd had. I'm encouraged to even nurture them. They are certainly not to be forgotten. I watch it and suddenly I'm present again, and I know that it was all real and that I'm real too, and the joy in my life is to treasure what good remains.

John C Stoskopf
Redford, USA

One common theme that runs in *Call Me By Your Name* is love. I, on the other hand, haven't experienced any, whether it is a heartbreak or falling in love. I'm 26 years old and I haven't had my first love. I think that's one of the reasons why I love this movie and book. I just want to thank you for making this movie.

Armie, I have been a fan since *The Social Network* and every time I see you on screen, I know I will be transported to a different dimension. This movie has touched me so much that I got the DVD, the book, and the soundtrack and shirts, too.

I want to know how it feels to be in love and also experience heartbreak and I want to be in love and receive love from anyone who would not judge my weight or the color of my skin. You have been an inspiration to all and I want to thank you from the bottom of my heart. You are truly an incredible human being and I'm thankful for joining this amazing wave! Peach gang forever!

Hawa Keelson 26
Cincinnati, OH
USA

I was actually living a wonderful life, until I saw *Call Me by Your Name*. I've never known any movie that moved me the way this film has done. It's been months since I saw it, but I can still feel the depth of emotions of every scene. This movie is a gift of a masterpiece. It has a very special power - so perfect that you will reminisce about the ups and downs of emotions you've felt back with your first love.

It'll make you sad, happy, complete and incomplete, all at the same time. The pain and sorrow of the last scene was just so magical, it still lingers. I think this is the only movie in recent times that made all moviegoers glued to the big screen through the end credits.

Also, it would be a sin not to commend Timothée Chalamet on his excellent performance as Elio. The day after I watched the film, I decided to grow my hair to look like Timmy. Later!

Joshua Guinarez
Manilla
Philippines

Call Me By Your Name has changed my life. For sure, the movie reminded us love is love is love. But more importantly, it gave me much more courage to continue my life.

I am 29 years old and live in Hong Kong. I have been having a really hard time recently. My beloved one is dying. He has a very rare and severe spinal tumor called Chordoma. After several recurrences, he is losing more and more functions of his body. The disease is almost sucking all the joy out of our lives. I was so lost and couldn't remember the meaning of life.

I suddenly time-traveled back to my teenage years and recalled so many details and feelings and words that I thought I'd forgotten. This tragedy brings me back to that time. I remember every single afternoon when I waited for him in the garden. I remember what he was saying. I remember his face, his smile, and his infinite love for me. I feel the warmest pain in the world.

Thank God this movie happened to me in my darkest day. I suddenly realized that these kinds of feelings were exactly what I should hold onto. The movie reminded me of the glory of all the beautiful things that ever happened to me. It gave me more courage to embrace those unexpected or unpredictable things that might happen to us in the future.

We all might get something really bad in our lives. But if we're lucky enough, we also could get something really good and beautiful. At least we've already had some in the past. Now I can try to enjoy all the fascinating parts of life, including the joy and pain just like Elio did.

We felt the deepest pain of losing our love, even including a part of ourselves. We cried our brains out in front of the fire. But when we recalled all those beautiful moments we've spent together, we still couldn't stop smiling because that pain is the WARMEST PAIN in my life!!

Fion Zhang
Hong Kong

When I joined the *Call Me By Your Name Global Facebook Group*, it was just to find some other people who were as enthralled by the film as I was. I had a lot of questions and opinions. But a bonus was that I made so many friends from around the world!

Not only did we communicate through the Facebook page posts, some emailed me personally, some I talked to on the phone, and some I met in person. When people are feeling depressed, members give them hope. We share artwork, opinions, videos, and articles with each other. We talk about our lives.

These are people I never would have known if it had not been for our shared love of this wonderful movie. Each and every one has been supportive and loving. But I guess that is the point of the film, so I shouldn't be surprised!

Anonymous

I had my Elio and I had my Oliver. My Oliver was a conflicted boy I met in high school back in the 70's when it was unthinkable that two boys could have a life together. We carried on in secret for more than a decade, but he was filled with self-loathing and took that out on me, in spite of always coming back for sex when he felt the urge.

When I was finally ready to come out of the closet and find a life for myself in my late 20's, I pushed him away, so I wouldn't have to keep longing for the love that would never come. I hadn't seen him for thirty years until just last year, still holding him in my heart as I usually do with things I can't have.

I made a special effort to see him for two reasons. One: to see if there was anything still there, and Two: in the hope that seeing him again as he is now and not as the idealized boy I knew so long ago would free me from my crush. There wasn't, and it did. I no longer think of him daily and that's a good thing.

My Elio was a slightly younger man I met in college and had a brief affair with over a few months. Again, early 80's, so very much was in secret. He was a virgin and I was only a bit less innocent. He was the first man I fully made love to. Kissing had never even occurred to me before and I have never forgotten him. I was still obsessed with my Oliver at the time and so, mostly in fear of being discovered and exposed, I ended it.

We've seen each other a few times since - once for a night of lovemaking about five years after college and once he brought his partner to stay with me and mine at our house for a weekend (this time without any action). There was a reunion some years later when we almost ended up in bed, but something stopped me… which I kind of regret and kind of don't.

My husband fell ill with pneumonia right after I got home and nearly died. I would have blamed myself for my infidelity being paid back if he had. This year, I got a very sweet text from my Elio on Valentine's Day, telling me how much that first night we were together meant to him. I had forgotten that it had happened on Valentine's Day. I still feel a very strong emotional tie to him. I can't describe the feeling actually, but I think I wouldn't want to let him go again.

Last September, my husband died after a long fight with cancer. It's been a very trying time after 27 years of being part of something and now being only half of something. I'm doing okay, but that and a few other personal setbacks have left me pretty banged up.

Now comes *Call Me By Your Name*. I'm well past the age and well past the innocence of what Elio experiences in CMBYN. I know I'll never again have that kind of idyllic summer romance, but the movie and the book have given me the chance to relive those years of innocence and discovery and heartbreak, at least by proxy.

I've seen posts on Facebook by people who have watched the movie 10, 20, 30 times and more, get tattoos of peaches, buy shirts with Elio's silhouette, make fan-fiction art. Some of it very beautiful and some of it is kind of disturbing. I'm not obsessive about the story or the actors or the film, but it's had a huge impact on me and I've still got the Blu-ray sitting next to the player ready to watch again. I think I've watched it four times, once with Timothée Chalamet and Michael Stuhlbarg's commentary. I bought one of the enameled pins of Oliver's red trunks because I met my husband in a bar in West Hollywood called Trunks, so there's a tie-in.

I guess it's just fortuitous timing, but it's been a big help and I thank André Aciman, James Ivory, Luca Guadagnino, Timmy, Armie, Michael, Amira, Esther and all the other cast and crew very much for their work and for helping lighten up the darkest months of my life.

Anonymous
San Diego, CA
USA

"I can't stand the silence. I need to speak to you."

I'm totally messed up since I saw *Call Me By Your Name*. It was three weeks ago. Since then, I've watched the film four times and it's not the end, definitely. I've read the e-book and listened to the audiobook read by Armie. I've watched videos on YouTube regarding the movie and listened to that amazing soundtrack. I've ordered the paperback so I could take it anywhere and read those deeply heartbreaking pages any time I want to. I've joined a fan group on Facebook and even created an Instagram account for the purpose of following CMBYN & Timmy.

This is the first time. Never ever before have I felt like this. "Am I sick?" Am I so desperate with my own life if I totally dove into a life which doesn't belong to me?

Last weekend I took some friends to the cinema to watch *Call Me By Your Name*. None felt the same as I did after watching film for the first time. I completely, strongly and so deeply fell in love. I'm not quite sure if I love the film or the main actor or the chemistry. I haven't ever seen more beautiful kisses between men! Every scene is so full of passion and unsaid but clearly visible "things that matter." Or maybe everything together.

I thought it would pass somehow by itself. In other words, "to feel nothing so us not to feel anything – what a waste"! So, I let myself feel, so deeply feel. I started to hate that feeling, because all my days start and end with the weird feeling that consists of sadness and joy, misery and happiness. "How much sorrow can I take?"

Anyway, I'm glad I watched it and that it made me feel like this – I'm "not bankrupt", even though I'm over 30. I'm happy I joined this group too. I can see that I'm not alone by being crazy about "everything".

And lastly, this is the part, which made me cry for many days after:

"If you remember everything, I wanted to say, and if you are really like me, then before you leave tomorrow, or when you're just ready to shut the door of the taxi and have already said goodbye to everyone else and there's not a thing left to say in this life, then, just this once, turn to me, even in jest, or as an afterthought, which would have meant everything to me when we were together, and, as you did back then, look me in the face, hold my gaze, and call me by your name."

Ugne Jancyte
Vilnius
Lithuania

I recently visited New York City, where I love to see and report on the-atre, but I feel compelled to share my experience of seeing an extraordi-nary film in the Big Apple.

You know the expression "only in New York." Seeing a film in the Paris Theatre, a venerable art house cinema right off 5th Avenue facing the Plaza Hotel, can be an event. The 3:50 p.m. screening of *Call Me By Your Name* on December 16th was, for reasons I'm delighted to share, an event.

For one thing, the Paris has reserved seats, just like a Broadway theatre. The sound and projection are always perfect—something that doesn't al-ways happen just anywhere. And the star of the film, a 21-year-old actor named Timothée Chalamet, was scheduled to do a Q&A session after the movie.

Director Luca Guadagnino (*I Am Love, A Bigger Splash*) has created a work of art that has the nation's top critics falling over one another: The *New York Times, The Atlantic, Rolling Stone, The New Yorker, Vanity Fair*—the list goes on.

What are they gushing about? In one word, "Beauty!" (Remember actor Julian Sands coming upon a field of flowers (and Helena Bonham Carter) in 1985's giddily romantic "A Room With a View" and ecstatically uttering that word?) *Call Me By Your Name* brings that moment to mind.

The film is photographed beautifully, is exquisitely sensual, such that one almost feels the heat, the water, the cool marble, even the sweat on an arm. Mr. Guadagnino is known for the incredible palpable quality of his films, as well as gorgeously appropriate music. In fact, the entire film subtly seduces an audience and so beautifully that one loses track of time.

And slowly, reluctantly (they both have casual girlfriends), but inexorably, Elio and Oliver fall in love.

You may say, "Oh, it's a gay love story." In my opinion that is so reductive a viewpoint that it's sort like saying "Hamlet" is about a prince whose father is murdered, so the prince seeks revenge. Do you remember Lin-Manuel Miranda's now famous words he emotionally uttered when his "Hamilton" won the Tony Award the night after the Orlando nightclub murders? He said all he knew was "love is love is love is love is love" in a short poem he wrote for the occasion.

Tennessee Williams said, "A road can be straight, or a street, but human heart is curved like a road through mountains." Master essayist, novelist, and social critic Gore Vidal decried the human tendency to "label" everything to the end of his days. And yet we humans love to believe what we believe, despite all evidence and enlightened viewpoints to the contrary.

So, I give up. All right, we'll say *Call Me By Your Name* is a gay love story. But really, it's just a human story of intimacy and mutual empathy found.

The acting is exquisite; Mr. Chalamet (particularly) and Mr. Hammer are miracles of casting. The film is such a perfect storm of acting, direction, and photography that it seems to just exist.

Back to the Paris Cinema. After the film, which received an ovation from the audience, a moderator brought Timothée Chalamet onstage for discussion and audience questions. There were ushers to hand microphones to questioners. I hope you don't think that yours truly, moved as I was, could keep quiet.

Five rows from the front, I thanked Timothée for his courage and conviction (his talent is obvious and God-given) in playing this role. I said to him (and the audience) that I truly believed that this film would save lives. I used to be a high school teacher, and I know that teenagers are the highest risk group for suicide, gay teenagers particularly. Timothée seemed quite moved by my words.

At the end of the session I somehow found myself standing right in front of him (how could that happen?), and he graciously thanked me for my comments. I also asked a very nice young woman if she'd take a photo us.

This was not an ordinary afternoon at the movies, as you can see.

Manning Harris
Atlanta, GA
USA

It's just a movie they said. Not for me.

When I saw *Call me By Your Name*, I was expecting a happy ending. I needed to watch it again and again. I needed to understand every little detail in every scene, and it convinced me that my eyes were seeing a masterpiece.

Suddenly, the movie became not a refuge, not a fairytale with a happy couple that ended together forever and ever, but something real as real life, where there is passion, love, anger, sadness, where we smile and cry. And where I can get inspiration to carry on. To be strong, even in bad moments. To have a will to live - which is a little bit hard for anyone who has a mental illness like depression.

And now, I am meeting some incredible people who share the same feelings, in the place where we are free from any prejudice. And I think this is the biggest thing that a movie can leave to us.

Gustavo Onuki
São Paulo
Brazil

Seeing *Call Me By Your Name* in the theater was a very moving experience for me.

I was away at grad school in the 80's and going through a lot of self-discovery, while also learning to be an adult away from my family.

My upbringing had been the typical notion of college, marriage, children, and a happy life, just like everyone else had. During that first year, long suppressed feelings began to emerge, and, even though I continued to date women, I knew at some point I would have to explore this other side.

I took two whole years away from any type of dating or physical relationship. Basically, I just studied all of the time. It was an emotional purgatory, but easier than dealing with my real feelings.

The summer before my last year of school, I was approached by a man while I was shopping. At first, I thought he worked at the store when he complimented me on a tie that I was looking at. I got really uncomfortable when I realized that he was just someone who was shopping also. He asked me to join him for a cup of coffee, and that feeling of being mortified still returns to me as I remember that day.

Call Me By Your Name brought back some of these feelings for me. That strange mixture of confusion, infatuation, attraction, lust, love, heartache, and recovery is so extremely overwhelming at any age, but I feel it's worse when you are young.

I didn't live in a dreamy setting like Elio, nor did I have the physical beauty of the two actors, but the universality of the situation triggered an emotional response in me like no movie ever has before.

Many think this self-journey is easier for young people now due to same sex marriage and a greater acceptance than thirty years ago. I am not so sure. I think this can still be extremely difficult for people. One of the first men I was involved with couldn't admit to me that he was married with children. Once I discovered this, I called everything off. Later I would see him looking for affection in clubs, when he could sneak away.

After I read the book *Call Me By Your Name,* I started to remember him. I did some internet searches, spoke to a few old acquaintances, and discovered that he had committed suicide about 15 years after I had known him. I know that his upbringing had demanded that he have a wife and children. This memory came back to me when I heard Oliver tell Elio that he was getting married.

Call Me By Your Name makes me wonder many things. Did I ever have an all-consuming relationship like Elio and Oliver had? How would my life have been different? Should I have ever discussed my personal life with my father before he died?

But what it does most for me is transport me back in time to a younger self. I'd like to say to a simpler time, but only in the sense that I was naive. It was a complicated time - in a simple setting.

I'd like to thank the actors and the entire crew of the movie for a hauntingly beautiful story, and most of all, the author for a book that lingers with me unlike anything I've ever read before.

David Glassco
Chicago, IL
USA

Call Me By Your Name really changed my life. I have always been a shy person. I think I was just born bashful, so much so that I practically shake if I have to make a telephone call, even to a friend. I know it's not logical, but mental hang-ups seldom are.

I recently started a small business and did not have money to hire someone to do marketing. There were times when emails would not work, and I had to make the dreaded phone call. So, I took a couple of deep breaths and thought of Elio and his courage in letting Oliver know his feelings.

I repeated my new mantra – a variation of the line from the movie "It is better to speak than die… It is better to speak than die." I was so proud of myself! It gets easier every time I make a call. What have I been so afraid of?

Then, I tried it in my personal life. When waiting for a bus or after seeing a movie, I thought "Better to speak than die" in my head and was able to make small talk. Not a big deal for most, but a big deal for me!

Anonymous

I am 50 years old, was born in the Philippines, and grew up in Northern California. I have seen the film *Call Me By Your Name* twenty-seven times in movie theaters and I've seen it twelve times on DVD. I've even seen it while on vacation in Oslo, Norway! I have read the novel four times and I have had the pleasure of meeting the author André Aciman twice during his 2018 book tour: once in Seattle, Washington and once in San Francisco, California. I plan to fly to New York to see Armie Hammer's Broadway play in New York this summer, and I plan to visit Crema, Italy next summer.

Why has this particular story touched me so deeply? It all started in 1984 when I came out as a gay man to my father. Like Elio Perlman, I was a teenager and I enjoyed listening to new wave bands. I remember being so nervous about disclosing to my father that I was gay. And like Professor Perlman—my father reacted in a positive, nurturing and loving manner. He told me that he would always love me no matter what, and that he would always be proud of me. This conversation made a big difference in my life. It's had an impact that time cannot measure. I didn't fully realize how fortunate I was until much later, when most of my Filipino-

American friends who came out to their families experienced hatred and hostility. In fact, I still have friends who haven't talked to their parents in decades because of homophobia.

That's why I was so thrilled when I was recently able to show my father the film *Call Me By Your Name* at a family gathering. It was a cathartic experience for him to see the Perlman father-and-son scene and remember our own conversation back in the 1980's.

When critics say that parents like Sammy and Annella don't exist in the real world, I am quick to remind them that yes, they do exist. Fathers like mine are out there and their loving words set their children up for success by building self-esteem and self-worth. Parents like the Perlmans may have been rare in previous generations, but they are becoming more common with the growing acceptance of lesbian, bisexual, and transgender people.

This film has also touched me as a Jewish man. I converted to Judaism in 2005. I appreciate the intertwining of gay and Jewish identities in the story.

Today, I am an openly-gay, Jewish, Filipino-American elected official. I've worked in government for over twenty years and I have a partner of 26 years. In fact, he's just started calling me by his name! *Call Me By Your Name* is a constant reminder that a father and son conversation has the power to transform a life. Positive reinforcement and unconditional love make a huge difference. Ultimately, that's the message of this amazing film.

Robert Bernardo
South San Francisco, CA
USA

A friend of mine sent me a copy of the *Call Me By Your Name* audiobook last October 2017. I tried listening to it, but it was hard for me to understand it since it was my first time listening to an audiobook. The way that

André Aciman wrote it is not really your typical novel with simple words and sentences. I stopped listening to it. But then in November, I was browsing Facebook and I saw this article that *Call Me By Your Name* would be adapted into a motion picture.

My curiosity awakened my desire to listen to the audiobook again and give it another chance. So I started listening to it before I went to sleep, and I was hooked after the first ten minutes. Armie Hammer's voice was like music to my ears. He has this deep, seductive and very manly voice that weakens my knees and makes me fall in love with him.

I felt like I was Elio and Oliver was reading it to me. I listened to it on my phone, even at the office. I finished it in 2-3 days. I honestly can't remember. What I can remember is that after the last paragraph, I couldn't stop crying like a child at my office table. I didn't want my officemates to worry about me and ask questions, so I went to the bathroom and cried again for another 30 minutes or more.

I was depressed for a week or two. I didn't have anyone to talk to because I don't really have any gay friends or even really close friends to share the story with. I live in a small city and most of my friends hadn't heard of it. I seriously and literally watched the film trailer every day as soon as I woke up and I could memorize the lines while *Mystery of Love* by Sufjan Stevens is being played!

The way Armie Hammer said the words "Call me by your name and I'll call you by mine" is euphoric. It brings me to another dimension that I can't explain. I cry every time I remember Elio and Oliver and that summer "somewhere in Northern Italy." It was like I was with them the whole time.

It's like a part of me died after the last paragraph of the story.

I made a lot of friends from all over the world because of the movie. We share the pain, the love, the lessons and the experiences we've had and how much we can relate or are affected by the movie and the book.

I read the e-book version, but I just knew that I needed to have a physical copy. It's the first book that I bought with my own money, so it's really special to me. I read the book once and I kept it inside my closet, like my bible. I also downloaded and listened to the *Call Me By Your Name* album EVERY DAY because I love it so much, especially the songs of Sufjan Stevens - *Futile Devices, Mystery of Love* and *Visions of Gideon.*

When the time came that the movie was finally released here in the Philippines, I traveled more than six hours just to watch it, because it was a limited release and the big cinemas didn't show it. It was only available for three days. I watched it alone and with a small audience of less than 20 people. I was silently crying starting from the peach scene when Elio said "I don't want you to go" up until the last part where Elio is staring at the fireplace while *Visions of Gideon* is playing. I can't put into words how deeply affected I was by it.

I personally don't have a story related to the movie, but I just feel like it's real and I feel like I was Elio. It's one of the best stories I've ever read or watched. I don't watch it very often even though I already have a copy of the movie because I want to cherish every time I watch it and that it feels new again whenever I watch it.

Thank you, André Aciman for making this masterpiece and thank you Luca Guadagnino, James Ivory, Timotheé Chalamet, Armie Hammer and the rest of the amazing cast and crew for making this story come to life.

P. S. I'm planning to go to Crema someday and who knows? I might find my Oliver there :)

Chris Dave Tan
Philippines

I would like to personally thank all involved in the making of this film for your effort and your passion. I hope all our voices will be heard and those who like me who have suffered the tragic loss of their first love. I have no idea how to start. I have no idea how to fit all my emotions. So here is my part:

This book and film have brought back so many memories from my past. So many similarities of the persona of Elio. Falling in love with "my Oliver". The life-changing experience of the first love. As others have said, I can't get this film out of my head. Bringing memories back, when I lived in northern Italy, my mornings of peaches, the nights I called his name and the pain of the loss of that first love. They say first loves are not meant to be, but as our main characters love each other and will so on, so will I remain in memory of that love. Call me by your name and I will call you by mine. Pasquale!

P.S. I only want to have a voice in life and not be someone who is invisible.

Paschalis

I attended my first viewing of *Call Me By Your Name* not knowing what to expect. It was an anxiety filled two + hours because I was sure that someone was going to either get sick or die.

When the film was over, I sat there through the credits until the screen went black and joined in the spontaneous applause with tears in my eyes.

It was my second and many subsequent viewings that allowed me to not only enjoy this work of art, but to digest a bigger message.

I am a 64-year-old, mostly closeted man. I could relate to Oliver and his feelings of obligation to be what society required. I too had an encounter and while it was nothing as romantic as what Oliver and Elio had, it was a great friendship.

But in the 1970's, being gay was not an option for most, and there were certainly no role models, just the stereotypes in the media at the time. So, I too took the road mostly traveled and got married and had a couple of kids. Unfortunately, my marriage ended, (perhaps it was doomed from the start, who knows?)

Once I was divorced, I allowed myself to explore my gay self. After a wonderful three-year relationship, and subsequent shattered heart, I found myself getting custody of my two kids. This would not have happened if anyone knew I was gay, so the closet door was shut and locked.

My kids are fully grown and have their own lives, and yet, I still find it impossible to tell them that I am gay. I have been alone for the past 20 years.

Life is short and *Call Me By Your Name* has made me realize that "I have wasted so much time".

So, I am in the process of purging my house, and selling a place I have called home for the past 24 years, and will be moving to Asheville, NC in the hopes of meeting another senior guy who wants a partner to journey with, for however many days we have left.

I am determined to just put myself out there and hope for the best. As for my kids .... I will tell them, when there is something to tell. *Call Me By Your Name* has been life-changing for me. Mr. Perlman's speech is something I wish I had heard 40 years ago. But I have heard it now ... and I am finally moving forward.

W. J. Tilly
Poughkeepsie, NY
USA

Call Me By Your Name is a story that has not only captured my eyes, but also my heart and soul.

I first discovered CMBYN through coming across trailers of the film. I watched one, and a part of me became so interested in seeing it. I then discovered it's actually based on a book, and I didn't really want to watch it until I read the book because I usually don't like watching film adaptations of books without having read the books prior to that.

Time passed, and I kept seeing *Call Me By Your Name* pop up in various places online, and I knew that there was something really truly special about it, but I still hadn't read the book. I finally got a copy of the book and read it, after months of not being able to do so because I was busy with college. I absolutely loved the story!

First of all, there's just so much emotion and intellect in the novel that really captured me so, so much. I honestly felt like crying reading certain parts of the story, and that rarely happens whenever I read books, even books that I really like. Secondly, without going into too much detail, it has really touched me on a much deeper level.

While I haven't been through the exact same experiences as Elio and Oliver in the story, I can still relate to them in such a profound manner (mostly Elio, but then I look back on the story, and Oliver's quite relatable, too). I say this because the story not only reminds me of my past, but also my present. Even though I don't have all the intellectual skills and talents of Elio, I can say that I really relate to his longing and desire to be with Oliver; the joy and the sorrow that strikes his heart.

I watched the movie as soon as I finished reading the book, and again, I loved it so much. The cinematography is brilliant, the soundtrack's wonderful, and the chemistry between Timothée Chalamet and Armie Hammer as Elio and Oliver really is touching to watch.

Mystery of Love by Sufjan Stevens pulled on my heartstrings, especially when they chose to play that song in the actual movie. The lyrics are so poetic, and the melody is beautiful. The song perfectly tells the story of Elio's love for Oliver, capturing both the joy Elio feels and the sorrow he eventually feels later on in the story wonderfully well. I honestly get chills whenever I hear that song. Just listening to the melody really affects me.

JC _1997
Manilla
Philippines

How did *Call Me By Your Name* change my life? It changed my life and my perspective. Before you love someone, you must first find your comfort zone. It is not all about a love story. It has so many things to say. It is trying to teach a lesson for someone who can't come out from the closet. When it comes to loving, no one can stop you from being in love.

Red Concepcion
Manilla
Philippine

There are so many movies that we watch, but only a few make us think and fewer that leave an impact.

This film hits us, and the impact will last forever. It's something that we can never get enough of, like a drug. After watching *Call Me By Your Name*, I told my friend that my heart broke and that I didn't even know that I had one.

I've never used "heart" in a context. I was the person who always said that there is no heart and there is just mind. The only thing that I wanted to feel was happiness and I had turned all the other emotions down. It was a process of years that had made me feel nothing.

It all started three years ago. After surviving cancer twice, the third time my dad passed away. It was not even a month after I had turned fifteen. It was my mother who was most affected. I had lost my father, but she had lost her love and life. She cried every day and every night. It was so painful to see her like that. It was so painful to see my papa dead, it was so painful to see him covered in blood, it was so painful because the person who gave me life was lifeless and that day I understood the true meaning of death.

36

Lots of people visited us and every time someone mentioned my dad my mom started to cry. She also cried when she saw someone crying. I tried telling everyone to not cry in front of her or talk about my dad, but who would listen to me? I was just fifteen. I had decided to not cry or talk about my dad with my mama. I suppressed all my emotions.

Initially it was for my mom, but soon I had started doing it for my sake. Not feeling the pain felt better so I killed the pain. I didn't cry for one whole year. I saw myself growing faster, maturing faster than people around me. After one year I had to break the piled-up emotions, even if it was just for few minutes. I shut it down again. It was not like I never cried. I used to cry, but for the things that didn't matter, things that didn't hurt so much. I used to cry when I saw someone crying. But as I was getting closer to seventeen I stopped that too.

It was the week of my seventeenth birthday and also during my final exams that my grandmother passed away. I knew it was going to be hard, I knew I had to cry. After hearing the echoing sounds of people wailing for hours, after watching my ammamma (granny) lying there dead, I didn't shed a tear. My mind was numb, and I had to take my final exams. I screwed up all my exams and had to break down for an hour.

I brushed everything off again. These hard times demanded the tears that I couldn't offer. After one whole year, one night for the first time I was listening to *Mystery of Love*. It was two weeks after watching *Call Me By Your Name*. After listening to this song repeatedly and envisioning Elio and Oliver through the song, I broke down and started crying. It was again the time of my final exams, after one year. I was constantly listening to the same song for days and weeping for hours; it broke me.

Call Me By Your Name broke the shell that I had built. I was finally crying, crying for Oliver to come back, perhaps I was crying for my Papa to come back, crying for my ammamma who deserved to be remembered. I was crying to feel alive, I was crying to feel the pain and dive into it and to compensate for the years of running from it.

Even after all the weeping, I did better in my exams than the previous year. It taught me that, it was not the pain which numbed me, it was not expressing the pain which did. I only wanted to feel the happiness and there was nothing wrong in it. But feeling happy doesn't mean shutting all the other emotions down.

Happiness, pain, fear, joy, sorrow, excitement, anger, etc. are all the emotions that make us human. They are all equally important. *Call Me By Your Name* made me more human. The perfect blend of all these emotions is love; I was running from it, too. I ripped so much of myself to cure the things faster. It was Samuel Perlman's words that made me question all my choices.

Love brings so much pleasure, followed by a lifetime of pain. Love is complicated. At a point everything ends - the reasons could be anything, person, situation, death, etc. ... Perhaps it's not the love that ends, it's togetherness that does. By seeing the experiences of different people, by reading heartbreaking love stories, by listening to people share their heartache and by watching my mom cry every night, I had decided to not be with anyone. To stay away from relationships and love. Though I knew I would have no control over love, I also knew I had control over myself. I'm like the knight who doesn't speak.

I also enjoy being alone; it never felt lonely because I love solitude. By watching CMBYN, by watching Elio and Oliver falling in love and by the words of Elio's father, everything has changed. Every heartbreaking love story made me want to be celibate. But no matter how much *Call Me By Your Name* broke me, it made me want to be in love again. Not all eighteen-year-olds like being single; a lot of people think singlehood is miserable, but it isn't. Not all relationships are miserable, too.

Though *Call Me By Your Name* broke my heart, though the movie, the book and the song made me cry more than Elio, I still wanted that love. No movie had me weep and still made me want it more. That's how I started to understand that the pleasure is worth the pain. No matter how much pain one feels, the joy they felt would still be alive. I cry every time I listen to the songs, but I also smile by remembering everything that happened in northern Italy.

I don't run from pain anymore. *Call Me By Your Name* has taught me how to feel and nurse my pain instead of killing it. It showed me how amazing pure love is. It taught me that love has no labels and feelings are more important than the labels. It taught me the things that actually matter.

If I hadn't watched the movie, I would've been like Mr. Perlman. I would've come close, but something would've always held me back, as it always did. But now I'll be more like Elio, at least I hope I will. If I'll ever feel something as pure as Elio did for someone as pure as Oliver, I will speak.

I'm not yet ready for everything and I don't know what the future holds. If I'll fall into something so magical and pure, I won't run from it. I'll let my someone call me by their name and I'll call them by mine.

Gangothri Ladegaam
Hyderabad
India

When I first saw the film, I wasn't expecting much. I really, really enjoyed it that first time, but my obsession kind of crept up on me in the weeks after. I couldn't get it out of my head. I watch a lot of movies and some of them are great. But this was something else, some kind of all-encompassing, beautiful haze that is difficult to describe.

I thought about it constantly and was strangely tense. I've searched every corner of my mind to figure out why I'm so enveloped in it, because I've never felt this way. I see myself as a level-headed, not an easily moved person. But now, I became myself as a teenager, like when I used to put posters of boys up on my wall in the 90's.

We had a bad winter, and it seemed summer would never come. Maybe that had to do with it? I'm still not sure, but one of the answers I came up with, as to why I couldn't stop thinking about it, was the feeling of being there, in Crema in the 80's. That whole world, with its sounds, images, and the way the script was written and the direction and how the actors played it and the costumes. Now I'm just listing every aspect of the film! But I love everything about it.

If you can fall in love with a film, as if it were a person, then that is what has happened to me. It's a wonderful feeling. When I told a friend about my obsession and said I was a bit embarrassed about it, he said isn't this the meaning of life? To fall in love with art!

Joanna
Malmö
Sweden

So how did the film and book *Call Me By Your Name* affect my life? When I first saw the trailer, it grabbed my attention, not because of its subject but by its look. The lazy summer and the gentle music. Then I realized American actor Armie Hammer starred in this film. I liked his work in *The Social Network*, so I had to see it.

Before I saw the movie, I started reading the novel by André Aciman. I was absorbed so much in the story of Elio and Oliver, I couldn't put the book down. Then I saw the movie on Christmas Eve. Bang! I felt I had woken up. I experienced so many emotions. I was a blubbering mess, sitting in the car after the film.

Thanks to the novel and film of *Call Me By Your Name*, I now go out of my way to watch independent films, so I no longer feel emotionally numb after I see a film. The story of Elio and Oliver has woken me up to my past and my current state of emotions. Thankfully, I found a Facebook group *Call Me By Your Name Global*. There I can see I'm not alone. So, I say thank you to André Aciman for your gift and thank you to Luca Guadagnino.

Beky Tully-Gibbens
Melbourne
Australia

It was January 1st when I watched *Call Me By Your Name* for the first time. As a cinephile, I'm used to lists and I made it my number one movie of the year.

Read the book ... Listened to the audiobook ... and started following this amazing group of CMBYN lovers.

Eliana Franco
São Paolo
Brazil

SONNET TO OLIVER

(For Armie Hammer and Timothée Chalamet)

The room is gone, and so are you who stands
Quietly by this balcony, dreaming
Of one who dreams upon your bed, with hands
Grasping, if only in sleep partaking
Of that embrace which only you can give him
Seek him, take him, round the proud monument
Of war and of the solemn dead, the dim
Light of morning on your face, the moment
Frozen into place, this space of silence
And if this dream of a dream beckons you
Back from distant shores, only his presence
By your side will remind you, that two
Souls parting by the whistle of a train
Is beyond love, beyond sleep, beyond pain

Thomas Pe
New York, NY
USA

SONNET TO ELIO

(For Timothée Chalamet and Armie Hammer)

Often I have looked at you with mine eyes
The furtive gaze, the nervous glance, they all
Hide what the heart can see, what truth there lies
Beneath my solemn calm of quiet, call
Out your name, and my restless soul anchors
Into still waters, cold from the mountains
We have trod together, like safe harbours
After a storm, or the cool of fountains
Under green arbours, where you held my face
To spread solace on these, my parted lips
And kissed me, I remember still this place
Long after summer died, long after ships
Of deep remembrance have borne you away
(To where, I cannot say) I will not stay

Thomas Pe
New York, NY
USA

I am, as the French say, "a woman of a certain age". My husband died years ago, and I have not dated much since. I really thought I had lost my sexual desire and was resigned to be celibate the rest of my life. This movie did what I thought was impossible: the sex scenes were so erotic that I rediscovered a libido that I thought was gone forever.

When I left the theater, I just wanted to grab the next person I saw and make out! I joined an online dating site for seniors. My children, who have been urging me to do this for years, are thrilled!

Anonymous

Call Me By Your Name changed my life.

I live in Sweden and I visited the places where *Call Me By Your Name* was shot with three friends in April. I went by train: Bologna-Fidenza, Fidenza-Cremona and Cremona-Crema.

It was the third time I visited Italy, but the first time I traveled by train there. The trains were late and there was nobody to turn to, so it became difficult.

When I arrived in Crema, I was pleasantly surprised. There was not one person waiting for me, but three. I did not know anything about these people; we had never had contact before. Francesca Gnocchi of Pro Loco Crema organized a meeting between me and these three people. It was an unforgettable experience!

We spent one day together that seemed like a movie. We visited Piazza Duomo in Crema, Piazza Vittorio Emanuele in Pandino and the Fontanile Quarantina in Capralba. I organized everything so that a taxi driver would take us everywhere.

The day ended with us eating croissants with apricot filling in Piazza Duomo in Crema. That was a day that I will remember forever, the day when I met some friends who shared with me the love for the same film. I've never had a similar experience in my life!

Now I have contact with three people, two who live in Crema and one person who lives in Lyon, whom I would never have met without the movie *Call Me By Your Name*.

Damian Ajvaz
Uppsala
Sweden

After watching the movie, aside from being depressed and saddened, I felt desperate to be in love. I was desperate to find my Oliver or at least desperate to find someone who's gonna comfort you when you need it the most and someone who's passionately in love as the way you do. I was so hopeless that night to the point I rushed myself to find that guy instead of waiting for me it to come. I craved for an Elio-Oliver kind of relationship.

Before I slept that night, I installed Grindr, SKOUT, Kik & Tindr on my smartphone and started creating accounts and chatting with some people. After a couple of weeks of conversing with some people, I realized that it wasn't the right place for me to find real love. I wanted love, not sex. No offense to all its users and not to generalize but most of the people I've known in that apps were looking for the "right now" moment. Sex without love is not satisfying. But who knows? We can't tell. Rihanna said, "We found love in a hopeless place". So, I decided to stop. I decided to not uninstall the apps, either.

That being said, for a few days, I lost my interest in watching porn videos. Which I think is good for me knowing that involving such actions is a wrong. I was a saint for a couple of weeks. I never looked at the boys the same way again. I didn't see them as "walking-dicks" for a few days. At that moment I realized, for a short span of time, I was being true to myself and I felt very sorry for myself. I was really looking for a real love and not lust. Not for a family love, nor a love coming from a friend but a lover's love.

The word change does not always mean turning from being bad into good. Most people I've known, who have watched the movie, they said they were changed by the film. I wonder, was it from worse to better or the other way around?

I'm not blaming the movie, but I'm blaming my actions instead. I left my job after receiving a memo stating the I would be terminated if I came to the office late for the nth time. It is because I watched the movie again and again before I went to bed. It had been a ritual for a couple of weeks. So, I decided to resign instead of getting terminated. I mean, who wouldn't like to watch the movie and fall in love over and over again?

I already had plans of leaving that job a few weeks before, but that time I was triggered. Sad movies are not healthy for me, but I love them. I already got a new job. Plus, I am now reading the book *Call Me By Your Name* by André Aciman, the first book I ever bought with my own money. Also, I'm engaging in art now, which I have deprived myself of for almost a year now.

I think a very important thing happened to me after watching the movie is when I joined the *Call Me By Your Name Global Facebook Group*. It is a group of different people coming from different kinds of life and who fully want is to share how deeply they fell in love with the movie and how it made them feel.

Finding this group is like saving myself from a suicide. Knowing that they have also felt the same way after watching the movie makes me feel like I am not alone. Someone who understands how saddened you are after watching the movie. It made me realize that sometimes being not okay is fine.

Anonymous

Watching *Call Me By Your Name* was, for me, nothing less than a life-affirming experience.

A pair of bright red swim shorts left out to dry, a sun-dappled peach plucked from a low-hanging branch, a hand resting gently but emphatically on another. Every single detail of this gorgeous film carries with it such immense power -- each one a reminder of the fleeting moments and the ephemeral things that make life so precious, creating memories to cherish that long outlive their subjects. Like an ancient statue brought up from the depths of a crystal blue-green sea, or a piece of fatherly advice that penetrates the heart and leaves one emboldened and inspired, this film is truly an embodiment of love - timeless, and yet incredibly timely.

I find myself longing to revisit this bygone summer often, with its leisurely bike rides, lush scenery, and newly-discovered passions that make the cold, dark winter that follows tremendously heartbreaking. Even so, as Elio's wounds become my own, I can already feel myself embracing the hurt and acknowledging that the beauty of what he -- and we viewers -- have experienced was worth the heartache.

The actors who brought these characters so vividly to life, and the creators responsible for making their world tangible, have touched me deeply. This film is something that has united us all, and something we will always share. For that, I am changed.

Madison Lee
Atlanta, GA
USA

I am a movie buff and have watched thousands of films in my life. But never has one affected me like *Call Me By Your Name*. When I left the theater, I felt like I was under a magical spell. As soon as I got home, I had to go online and find out more. It's been five months since I saw it, but not a day goes by that I don't listen to a song from the soundtrack, watch a fan video, or discuss it with someone. I've watched the movie over twenty times, read the book three times, and listened to the audiobook four times. Every time, I discover something new.

I am middle-aged, but I have become like a teenage fangirl, searching for interviews of all the actors. And now I am going back and watching all their previous films. Armie, Timothée, Amira, Esther, and Michael – you all were so wonderful in this and now I am enjoying all your other terrific performances. I look forward to seeing all your future films, too!

And thank you most of all to André Aciman for writing this beautiful tale!

Anonymous

Like many people, I was so deeply touched by this film. I can't recall a time when I was so emotionally moved by a story before. Timothée Chalamet and Armie Hammer brought these vivid characters to life so believably that by the end of the film, how could you not feel the heartbreak that Elio experienced? And also recall the same emotions from that crazy, confusing time in your own youth.

Besides the beautiful cinematography, amazing soundtrack, gorgeous production design and pitch-perfect acting, I was so moved by how Timmy and Armie embraced their parts in the publicity of the film. It was so validating to see two straight men so confidently embrace this love story and remind us all of how universal love is - no matter who you are.

Robert Stein
New York, NY
USA

I read *Call Me by Your Name* in September 2017. I heard of the movie and wanted to familiarize myself with this story. I fell in love with the novel when I read it. I wanted to be Elio, captivated by Oliver's charms.

When I finally saw the movie in late January 2018, I was elated. I was a 23-year old drawn to this story of a summer romance between two younger men in 1983 Italy. Sure, there were numerous LGBT films that came before *Call Me by Your Name*, but this one was groundbreaking.

Michael Stuhlbarg's moving monologue about his unconditional love and acceptance for his bisexual son towards the end of the film had me in tears. Maybe because I could relate to Elio and his budding feelings and sexual development is why that later scene between father and son hit me close to home. I wanted a father like Elio's father.

The final scene with Timothée Chalamet, as the credits roll, is heartbreaking, as he sits by the fireplace at Chanukah-time. The film ends with Elio looking directly into the camera, in European film fashion, about to face his parents with the woe that has overcome him. The camera goes to black.

The closing shot reminded me of Celia Johnson at the end of "Brief Encounter" (1945). The affair may be over, but the memories will subsist (whether good or bad).

Call Me by Your Name is one of those rare cases where I enjoyed the movie just as much as the book. They go hand-in-hand. They really do.

The novel and this film will stay with me for years and years to come. I hope many feel the same way.

Ben Koeberle
Clyde, NY
USA

One thing that makes *Call Me by Your Name* so inspiring to me is that I have since been able to make so many connections to it with other stories and films, particularly Disney fairytales. I'm a Disney fan, so it eventually wasn't much of a surprise when I began seeing connections with CMBYN to other Disney stories. CMBYN for one definitely reminded me of The Little Mermaid, both Hans Christian Andersen's original story and the version Disney decided to do (Andersen's actual backstory was about experiencing longing for another man, and the heartbreak he experienced with it being unrequited, hence the tragic outcome of the mermaid in the original fairytale).

But it also reminded me of *Beauty and the Beast*, especially the actual book. The sentiment of time really plays out in *Call Me By Your Name* just like in the story *Beauty and the Beast*. Elio reminded me of Belle, especially with him being a bookworm and his relationship with his father. Belle and Elio both call their fathers "Papa". I even thought of the song "Something There" at some point in the book when Elio and Oliver finally show their love for one another.

One final connection Disney-wise is regarding the controversial age gap between Elio and Oliver. A lot of people have been speculating on their age difference, saying it's "inappropriate", yet all the couples from the Disney Princess line-up, Rapunzel and Flynn/Eugene are said to have the widest age gap, and no one seems to judge that too harshly. Rapunzel is 17 and Flynn – according to the directors of Tangled – is said to be 24. So they basically have almost the same age gap as Elio and Oliver.

But it's not just in terms of Disney that makes *Call Me By Your Name* a reason to inspire/influence me. There are so many other interesting nuances and references in CMBYN that really capture my interest (the books Elio and Oliver read in the story, etc.), and I've learned so much from reading it (same thoughts apply with the movie).

A lot of other books that I've read, I usually just read, and then they're closed for a while, and I don't really go back to reading them again, so they've basically been "retired". But *Call Me By Your Name* is one book I'm still interested in rereading over and over again for everything– the emotions, the quotes, the philosophical ideologies, the literature references, and so on.

Call Me By Your Name is a story that has changed and inspired my life, and I hope it'll continue to reach out to others years from now.
JC _1997
Manilla
Philippines

I love the passionate affection between Elio and Oliver: it's so beautiful, genuine, and intimate. I admire Elio's courage to tell Oliver his feelings and how strong their love is for each other, although they know they will only have a few days together. It made me realize that the most important thing is to live now, in this moment. It has given me courage to do what I want in my life. I'm no longer scared to be myself, to say how I feel, and what I want. I have fulfilled my biggest dream and rented a small apartment just for myself. There I can say, "This is my spot. It's all mine." I would like to thank Luca, Armie, Timmy and the whole crew for this beautiful film and a wonderful experience.

Satu
Helsinki
Finland

A parent's perspective . . .

When I saw *Call Me By Your Name*, I was not prepared for the intense reactions I would have as the mother of a gay son. I felt jealousy, over-whelming guilt ...and in the end, was rendered speechless.

The scene that triggered my jealousy and guilt was Mr. Perlman's speech. I was so jealous of the relationship Mr. Perlman had with Elio. Why couldn't I have that kind of relationship with my son? Why couldn't I speak so eloquently with him about the things that matter?

Though I knew it would be painful, I watched the movie again. With this viewing, the jealously morphed into something far worse ...Guilt! When Elio was obviously hurting, Mr. Perlman didn't try to take away his pain. Instead, he encouraged Elio to hold onto that pain, and with it, the memories of a beautiful relationship.

When my son lost his first love, I wanted to ease his pain, negating his relationship, telling him he could do much better. The guilt stemmed from the fact that I had always vowed to be there for my children, and in this most vulnerable moment in my son's life, I was NOT there for him the way he needed me to be. I was failing Perlman Parenting 101.

Time passed, but the guilt remained until one day my son and I were discussing the movie. He said the drive home from the train station was one of his favorite parts because he felt that Elio's mom was there for him. I said I wished I could be like Elio's mom.

My son said nothing for some time. When he finally did speak, he said the reason that scene was one of his favorites was because it reminded him of us; he couldn't think of a time when I was not there for him. He said what he loved about that scene was that Elio's mom didn't need words (no speeches) to comfort Elio. Her presence was enough. He told me that scene pretty much defines OUR relationship …How I am always there for him. I was stunned. All I could do was take his hand and hold it. I had no words.

Anonymous
Dallas, TX
USA

When you're young and naïve and you think you're in control of life, you do a lot of things that you think are good, just because they feel good. No reason to question or doubt, just the bonus of youth. Foresight could sometimes prevent greater damage, or at least avert so far that you only scratch past with a small scrape. But it would have been just as easy as it is written here.

It must have been about 10 months ago when it all started. Or no, probably it was about 10 years ago, I do not know exactly. I cannot know that exactly. Nobody can know it. Too much has happened since then and it actually happened quite unnoticed. I cannot say that I was innocent, or in any way not negligent, or possibly uninvolved. It just happened, unspectacular and without much fanfare. And then it just lay dormant, secretly and quietly. Or rather, it rested in me.

I suppose I should have just said "No" when someone started all over again. The constant question of guys, whether with or without, was always one of the standard phrases that I came across again and again. No matter if the acquaintance existed for a few hours or if it was already of advanced nature, so that one could speak with some kindness of a kind

51

of relationship. In such, trust should be a mainstay, but what good is the greatest basic trust in a person who does not know himself? Or has deceived oneself, and many others before?

Did I fool myself? Did I lie to myself? Or did I just close my eyes? Locked up by reality, by the risk, by the madness that brought the whole thing with it. Maybe I lacked foresight and didn't care, but that's not important. Because now it happened, now the whole thing cannot be made back. Now I'm trapped in a spiral, because once you have it, you always have it. You can try to reduce and hide it, but it will always be there.

It did not just capture my body without me noticing. Well, at some point I did notice something: I felt more and more fragile, as I became weaker and weaker. Evidently so much that even those in my environment perceived a change in me and they asked me what diet I was doing.

Sometimes you just need external influences to open your eyes. When the result was finally clear, I would have liked to close them again. One fine day in the fall, I sat with the doctor, who looked at me with a look on his face, as if to say, "If you had hesitated any longer, you would not have experienced Easter." But finally he said to me, "If you had hesitated any longer, you would not have experienced Christmas anymore." All the harm, which came to light little by little, was as complex as a puff pastry: liver, lung, retina, intestine, blood, skin... day by day a new suffering. How much can you go unnoticed before it's too late?

But most of all, the virus did not do my head well. To carry one's own burden is one side. The other, perhaps to have burdened this burden flippantly with a fellow human being. And then the constant "why", the eternal "how did it come to that"? Like a fairground carousel, I turned more in circles with these trains of thought. Finding the exit, or an answer, is an impossibility. The sudden lack of prospects, which opened like a fissure, increased into a depressive pattern, which was difficult to break.

Get up in the morning, check. Open your eyes, check. Face the things, check. Tackle everyday life and work, check and check. To bring it to an end staying focused – a masterpiece when your own thoughts are always about one certain thing again and again. For many days I cried as soon as I felt unobserved, as soon as I entered my apartment or as soon as I was in bed. Often without immediate trigger, just like that. Sometimes for minutes, sometimes an hour, sometimes half the night. In the company of friends I made no sound, couldn't follow the many conversations, every word was too much. And words were just futile devices anyway. Trapped in a swamp that completely encased me and pulled me lower and lower.

On one of my better afternoons I visited the local cinema on the advice of a friend. A nice try to cheer me up and bring people together. Now I have never been a fan of mainstream movies and would have preferred to cancel if I was not simply dragged along. I am still very grateful for that today. Because it was not an average blockbuster that I would watch; no, it was something completely different. It was not just a movie. It was as if I were looking back at my own life through the screen, at my youth, retrospectively.

Like a spectator of a particularly beautiful exhibit in a museum, I was intrigued by its nature and the fact that my past and his present seemed eerily similar. A flash directly from my youth in the 80's, right in the middle of the here and now. Elio, whom I am now watching, and Daniel, whom I now recall, seem one and the same person.

Though I grew up somewhere in northern Westphalia, had dark, curly hair, loved music, arts, enjoyed the sun evermore. Back then I was not unfamiliar with the fact that I was more interested in boys than girls. But there was never a concrete addressee for my desire. No one to release my inner handbrake. All my desire, my devotion, I used to keep it for myself. Was it better to speak or to die? I would rather have died.

A long time later I would even, but for quite different reasons. For years I kept myself covered, almost hidden. Meet like-minded people? No way. How should one say openly what one would like if what one wants is frowned upon? If what you want, nobody else wants? If all advise against it. Would I ever know the mystery of love? Did I want someone

53

to know? And if he finds out, am I done? Oh God, my parents. The family, everyone!

So when I was trapped in the cinema chair, I felt so connected to Elio. All these sensations culminated and overturned; emotions that were long since ticked off raged in me all of a sudden. Because apart from all the obvious parallels and similarities, there was one significant difference. Why could I never experience what Elio experienced? Why was I taken what Elio was given? Why was not my environment so tolerant? So open-minded and intellectually able to constructively deal with other things and be good, instead of rejecting them unchecked and without questioning them. Why did everyone else always know what's better for me than myself? Why can't I turn back time? Would I, then, with my experiences today, do things differently? Would I be more open, would I be freer, would I be more alive? Would not I have the virus then?

Elio's insecurity, his inner restlessness, his burgeoning, insatiable desire, his secret devotion and passion are parameters that set me apart at the age of 17, just like him. How much would I have wished for an exchange student who abducted me into worlds that I would at that time have dreamed of entering? How much I would have liked parents to give free rein to their child's feelings, feelings and inclinations, rather than taking them seriously, stopping them and even trying to screw them back. How fast is one too old and emotionally bankrupt and then has nothing left to invest? How quickly is one's own body unattractive to others? Sometimes not for reasons of age.

Rarely has a film and its message touched me more. Seldom has a movie been such a balm on my soul and raised so many questions in me and answered them at the same time. Each time I watch it, it feels like watching a private holiday video from my own past. Of course it's just an illusion, but one that pays off. A vision from another world at a time with comparatively small worries. An escape, a refuge.

Countless times I have lost my mind somewhere in northern Italy now. I took part, was happy, I longed, laughed and I cried all at once. Which therapist can do this in two hours? Meanwhile, for me the sky is blue again and the trees bear their leaves again. I know again that life can be as light and airy as a bike ride into the countryside. With Elio I am just relaxing. Standing at the abyss, AIDS nearly ruined me over the years. In no time, Elio rebuilt me. A brother, an ally, a soulmate. A second self who also had to suffer. But many wounds heal with time. A time Elio helped me to come. Today my doctor said, "You don't need to come as regularly as before. See you at Christmas", and I grinned. Thank you for the time you lent me, Elio.

Daniel Koeneke
Germany

Call Me By Your Name reflects everything I've ever wanted to experience in a movie, especially the way the love story is embodied and developed: the meeting, every single act that witnesses the feelings of the characters, the longing for the loved one...

I think there's a before and an after *Call Me By Your Name* for me, as this story taught me desire and love, and made me understand how I want to feel in a relationship. I'd like to love someone the way Elio and Oliver love each other: with full respect, devotion and admiration, your soulmate being the one raising you up and helping you believe in yourself at the same time.

I could spend days looking for the right words to express how deeply moved I was by this movie. The whole combination of such beautiful, contemplative and intellectual emotions, and such perfect characterization makes this movie a unique artistic and spiritual experience in life. And you just want to be part of it and make it last forever.

There's not much to say but thank you, to Luca Guadagnino, to Timothée Chalamet, Armie Hammer and all the cast of the movie, to Sufjan Stevens who is the most incredible composer I've ever listened to, and to André Aciman especially, whose words about defining love and desire I'll never forget.

Camille De la Chapelle
Paris
France

One camera. One script. One cast. One Italy.

Do you remember the feeling when you meet someone interesting and that person touches you for the first time? The inner shiver, electrical storm under your skin, running down to your stomach and freezing every neural process in your body? Yes, it's pretty much the universal feeling after watching *Call Me By Your Name*. But why?

It's the way Luca films things. So close. So careful. In a way, we are every book, every road, every food and every peach in the movie. When they go swimming, we are the water. When they walk around, we feel the sun and the wind. Luca created an environment that allowed us to *become* Italy.

And once you are Italy, these two gentlemen come inside your world and develop the most delicate relationship, full of unsaid words and ambitious desires. It's the way Timotheé Chalamet charms his French through Elio, fascinating people with his blasé look. It's the way Armie combines vulnerability and assertiveness into Oliver, feeding our protests at each "Later!" It's the way both trespass their own limits into a higher surrender.

It's the way the curves of their bodies challenge us to desire them. The intoxicating yearning to touch each other. The words, finding safe swings. "You know what things…"

Lastly, when the love feast is over, and all we have in the room is Elio's tears … soon we are the fire raging against the dying of the light. Sufjan Stevens pulls his last card, his royal flush. Timotheé looks right into us and Sufjan asks, "Is it a video?"

You could say so, but none of us felt this way.

It was not a video. It was a masterpiece.

@CardiBiz
São Paulo
Brazil

I already knew I was gay since I was in grade school, but I didn't come out. I'm still in denial and I'm afraid of rejection by both society, around my family and friends. Just like Oliver, I'm bound to do what is normal in the eyes of society and at the same time envious of Elio because of his almost perfect life with supportive parents and friends, and his confidence in himself.

I am grateful to have watched the movie, as it was an eye opener for me to embrace my sexuality. I'm already 34 and feel so empty because of this excess baggage that I am carrying almost my entire life. I think I deserve and need to give myself a chance to be happy. I think letting this go can release me from this burden and depression.

The movie gave such valuable lessons to me. It touched me to the core, inspired me to love and be loved in return, to be who I am and accept the fact that I am indeed not of the norm. The movie served as a reminder to be determined and confident in myself, being able to express wholeheartedly to my family and friends. All I need to do now is to have the courage to reach out to my loved one and come out as this is the only reason to be free and happy.

Anonymous
Dubai
United Arab Emirates

There was no context. No pre-cursor. No research done. When I walked out of the theater, my heart was broken. My mind was filled with memories of euphoric, joyous summers. My body: chills up my spine, my face burning red, and tears streaming down my face.

Although I've had countless interactions with those who have also been touched by the film, I have not shared one aspect that is reflective of myself. I come from a strict immigrant household where the concept of homosexuality was one of sin and misunderstanding. Although I came out to my mother and brother beforehand, after watching the movie, it has given me an incentive and motivation to acknowledge my father. Although he is tougher to crack, I have learned that transparency and understanding is much better than silence, spoken ever so subtly by Annella, "Is it better to speak or die?"

At the age of 17, I was quite honestly dumbfounded at my lack of intelligence and cultural interests after seeing Timothée Chalamet's performance of Elio. I was inspired by the fact he learned Italian and the piano for this role. I am now immersing myself within the elements of the movie: I have enrolled in a philosophy course, started indulging in European history, started to teach myself piano, and picked up inspiration for outfits this summer.

Overall, the film has allowed me to open up multiple perspectives in which I can grow upon. It has solidified my understanding that love is love, regardless of who it is between. I can finally push myself to open up to my father. Finally, I am able to balance a healthy mind with a healthy heart. I will forever be indebted to this movie and cast for changing my life, and for that, I will be forever grateful.

Gabriel
Chicago, IL
USA

Call Me By Your Name ruined my life and I love it.

Well, my life as I knew it. I've never been so disturbed and affected by a movie or book before, but it's the best feeling I've ever experienced.

When I heard about the book (a tip from a journalist that I long admire), I was captivated by the title but in the end, it was the movie that I saw first, and I'm glad I did. Watching the film without knowing much about it, just made the whole experience more intense. It was mind-blowing. Suddenly, I was overwhelmed by some sort of emotional storm. I remember going to sleep in tears that day. I spent a whole week feeling completely depressed.

Then I read the book and felt like an emotional wreck and I was heartbroken and obsessed by the story. It was like being under a spell; I couldn't get it out of my head. I lost count of how many times I've watched the movie. And I keep re-reading the book. Feeling all over again. "Sweet torture" as one fan said.

No, I don't have a heartbreaking story of a lost love. Maybe I wish I had, because I feel like I've never experienced a love as deep as that of Elio and Oliver's. And what a beautiful love story it is. The most beautiful I've ever seen. While watching the film, I felt like I was falling in love myself. I felt the tension, the angst, the butterflies in the stomach, everything.

Suddenly summer became my favorite season, blue skies gained new colours, and I wished I could live in *Call Me By Your Name*, spend lazy summer days riding bikes, reading books, playing music ...all those simple pleasures of life now have more meaning than ever.

I fell in love with Elio Perlman. He's become my all-time favorite fictional character. How I love his braveness, and yet he is so sensitive. He's not afraid of showing his emotions or exposing his vulnerabilities. Such a complex and endearing boy.

There's a feeling of deep melancholia that takes over me every time I watch the movie or read the book. A sense of grieving. Maybe because *Call Me By Your Name* reminds me of everything I put away, everyone I left behind, every dream I've ever given up whether I hadn't had the courage to pursue it or because life stood in the way. I feel like my "Oliver" is everything I ever loved and have lost.

It also made me think of time lost. Time is so cruel. And after all, it left me with a sense of urgency to live. I never felt so alive. It was like waking from a numb state of mind. I feel like I had been so cynical about love and about so many things, that now I don't want to be like that anymore. CMBYN made me want to live my life in its fullness.

Since I've become a "peach", I started playing the piano again after many years, I'm enjoying photography (not just selfies), I'm reading a lot more, I like riding bikes like never before, I'm writing a journal, I've learned macramé techniques (yes, I wanted to make those Elio's friendship bracelets), I'm saving for a trip to Italy (life goal) and, best of all, I've met the most amazing, interesting and lovely people in the world, my peach friends. I found someone to talk about "the things that matter".

I will be forever thankful to Mr. Aciman for have written this marvelous novel with such amazing characters, and also Mr. Ivory, Luca, Timothée (never an actor had made me cry so hard in my whole life), Armie and everyone that made of CMBYN this sensitive, beautiful and inspiring masterpiece.

Call Me By Your Name owns my heart and will always be with me.

Daniella Neri
São Paulo
Brazil

I am a 63-year-old Hungarian woman and I have two children. I was married for 30 years and as it often happens, my husband found a younger woman and left me. That was 14 years ago.

I was 18 when we met, and I thought it was the best choice of my life to marry him. I made a big mistake, but it does not matter anymore.

Since then I had one longer relationship, but now I live alone but I don't feel alone because I have a lot of friends and a grandson who makes me happy.

I watched the movie mid-February and from that time my life changed in so many ways. It is ridiculous, but I fell in love with Timothée in such a way you cannot imagine. I have feelings I thought I never had. I got addicted to everything in connection with *Call Me By Your Name*. Videos, interviews, magazines. I am obsessed with the two guys and I can tell you that I have never seen such a beautiful love story in my life. Moreover, I wasn't in love with anybody in such a way as Elio.

It makes me very sad to know that I won't get love back, so I watch the movie almost every day and try to be happy and not to cry.

Anonymous
Budapest
Hungary

I'm a gay man who comes from an Italian family. My family had always embraced their heritage through cuisine, loving Italian filmmakers and artists, and attending Italian festivals. Unfortunately, they have been horribly abusive and neglectful towards me since I was five years old. Because of that, anything Italian-related always felt tainted to me. Every time people would ask me what I was, and I told them I was half Italian, I never felt proud, because my family made me such an outcast.

However, when I first saw *Call Me By Your Name*, I forced myself not to feel that same tainted feeling as before. I didn't want the memories of my abusive family to take away of what this film had to offer. I didn't want to diminish the experience while watching it, especially since I love all aspects of cinema and filmmaking and love to be immersed when watching films. I've also always been a deeply romantic person and I wanted nothing to hold me back while watching this love story unfold.

And in a weird way, it worked.

Despite how the family I had come from loving their Italian heritage, I barely knew anything about Italy. This film showed me a side of Italian culture that I hadn't seen before, such as the passion when the language was spoken, the settings, and the food. More especially when I later read the book.

"Culture" may be too strong of a word, and no matter how romanticized or glorified the film and book made it out to be, it offered a different perspective nonetheless. It was as if that tainted feeling deep in my stomach was finally gone. Like I gained a missing part of myself back, like that wound that my family left me was now healed. I no longer felt the resistance when speaking, reading, or watching anything related to Italy.

A few months after seeing the film (three times in theaters over the span of a few weeks), I read the book. Halfway through the book, I began reading it out loud, including reading the Italian words and phrases (but of course failed miserably) and it felt good.

While there are plenty of films, music, and books that always resonated with me and made me feel less alone, nothing ever had such an impact as this. Through everything the film and book had to offer, this cathartic journey allowed me to let go of the darkness my family left me in, so I could see the world and myself in a brighter way.

Grazie mille to André Aciman, and everyone involved in creating this film.

Anonymous
California
USA

I saw the film on January 1st, and the obsessive pondering began immediately. I would dream about it and wake up crying all the time. I would break down regularly over the next three weeks, all the while admonishing myself to get a grip. I immediately read the book after seeing the film and consumed it in one sitting. My visceral reaction to the film (less so to the book, which I loved nonetheless) was mostly because it mirrored an event in my life 41 years ago.

I am a 61-year old Jewish gay man. In the summer of 1976, I attended a summer film workshop at Cornell University to work on a documentary on the bicentennial. The workshop was comprised of 15 college-age students from across the country. We all lived in a big house in Ithaca, New York, worked all day, spent all our evenings and nights together, and even regularly went to a nearby lake to skinny dip. It felt in so many ways like a carbon copy of that summer in Crema, minus our parents and with a bit less lounging around. Needless to say, we all got extremely close to one another, as only 19 and 20-year-olds can-- and, needless to say, I fell head over heels in love with one of them, one of the most gorgeous and sexiest men I had ever gotten to know in my entire life.

Greg and I became instant friends, and our relationship got closer and closer as the summer proceeded. I was so in love with him that it became hard to function. My stomach was always in knots and I couldn't get him out of my mind. Deep down I knew that he was interested as well (I saw the way he looked at me at the lake), and our close relationship was really progressing to a rather inchoate intimacy that neither of us had experienced before.

The problem, of course, is that I wasn't out yet (nobody was among all the people I knew at that time). No one at college had publicly come out yet; I would meet several a few years later in gay bars or on the streets of San Francisco - guys who, like myself, came out soon after (or in the final years of) college. But '76 was still a year (at least among the people I knew), perhaps even one of the last years in which young college-age kids were still largely closeted.

So here I was madly, agonizingly, in love and yet not out to my peers, and certainly not out to any of the kids in that film workshop (all seemingly straight). I simply didn't know what to do with all these feelings. It became more and more difficult to sleep - and one day it became so unbearable that I spontaneously made up this stupid story that someone had died in my family and that I had to immediately leave for Los Angeles. And so I did: I got on a plane and left. Of course, I regretted it the minute I landed in L. A. I excruciatingly grappled with that question that had so stirred Elio, "to speak or to die," and I hated myself for having chosen death.

I immediately approached my parents, who were of course quite concerned about my sudden departure from New York-- the reason for which I would not say. (I didn't come out to them until two years later.) I told them that I had made a terrible mistake and begged them to send me back. My mother, who was the "liberal" and more tolerant of the two, absolutely refused. She said that there's no way they would give me the money unless I told them what happened. I guess it was understandable that she would try to use this crisis as leverage to get me to come out to them. My father, homophobic and conservative to the core, completely floored me when he said: "It's none of our business. Yes, we'll send you. You don't have to tell us anything."

But here's the kicker. My grandparents were visiting my parents that day. And my grandmother, an old-world, Yiddish-speaking grandmother if there ever was one, took me to the next room and literally gave me the Michael Stuhlbarg speech. She didn't specifically mention sexuality or being gay, probably for the simple reason that I hadn't. She just told me in the strongest terms that I had to be myself and live my life the way I choose, and that I should never worry about what anyone thinks. She began talking about her brother, who had been married twice but ended up living alone and isolated in his later years. I assume she referenced him because he was a closeted gay man. Both she and my grandfather, whom I both loved with all my being, would be dead within a year. That talk was the most important thing she ever said to me.

So I went back to speak and not to die. And I spoke. I told Greg how I felt about him. His response was to say that that's okay and then proceed to start a sexual relationship with one of the women in the group (whom we both liked as a person, but whom we both knew he wasn't even remotely interested in). I kind of tortured myself for years that had I been a stronger and more self-assured person (that is, had I been more like Elio), his response would have been different. If only I had had the strength to simply seduce him, it would have been different. Why did I tell him as if it were some problem that we had to intellectually deal

64

with? Yes, Elio told Oliver as well, but I was so struck by how he didn't take no for an answer. I did.

I stayed for the remainder of the workshop, and during those final days confided what was going on to one of the film professors, a heterosexual man in his early thirties who was in a relationship with a wonderful woman. He confided back that a film that he had made (and that we'd all seen) about a close friendship in his teenage years was actually about a secret gay love affair he had.

One night a bunch of us-- Greg, me, the woman he was now sleeping with, and one other woman-- were lying on a bed talking and smoking a joint. At one point I put my hand on his thigh and held it tightly for what seemed like an eternity. He did not move away. That would be one of the most erotic experiences in my entire life.

Two years later, after I had come out, Greg came to Los Angeles and told me that he had wanted it as much as I did, but was too scared to act on it. By that time, he was in the middle of a committed relationship with a woman, so there was nothing we could do about it. It was water under the bridge.

So you can imagine how much this film pushed my buttons.

Anonymous
Los Angeles, CA
USA

I'm agonizing over this killer of a film because I deeply want to feel love in my life and experience the passion that Elio and Oliver personified. And I'm agonizing because I fear that (at 61) I'm too old to get that at this point in my life - a legitimate fear in this youth-obsessed world of ours, and one not to be brushed away with bromides that "you just have to put yourself out there more." It's tough. Perhaps the best I can do right now is simply be clear with myself that I haven't given up-- that I refuse to give up - and to treat myself as kindly as possible as I try to navigate the painfully difficult process of attempting to connect with someone in a meaningful way.

For quite a long time now, I've brushed aside queries about why I'm not dating anymore with disingenuous declarations that I'm no longer interested in all of that, or that I'm totally satisfied with creating a community of close friends (also not the easiest thing in the world when you reach a certain age, but that's another story).

I would hide behind cynical proclamations that the only older gay men out there who start relationships are those with lots of money who can buy love; that love's nothing but a commodity; that love's a mirage; that everyone is such a damaged package deal by a certain age that it's better not to bother with them; that I've already met my quota of getting involved with lunatics or sociopaths, thank you very much, and that it's so much better to be alone; and that, yes, what's the point when no one even wants to look at your body anymore, let alone touch it. All excuses. All convenient cop-outs to hide the fact that I'm scared of being hurt.

So I guess we are back to Professor Perlman's point about our heart wearing out and our being so scared to feel the pain. And I guess I have to keep telling myself that there is a clear choice before me: Surrender to the fact that life sucks and give up, or muster the courage to try again, knowing that the odds are stacked against you, and knowing that you might very well end up feeling like a fool for thinking things could work out in the end. But also knowing that you have nothing to lose.

Anonymous
Los Angeles, CA
USA

As a 61-year-old closeted gay man, professional, married to a wonderful woman for 30 years, with four grown children, this film has significantly impacted me. I reevaluated my whole life and may do things differently moving forward.

I even anonymously e-mailed a guy from high school that I had a secret crush on. He did not reply. In the south in the 70's you didn't talk about such things. I still don't know whether to come out or not.

Brian Zeller
USA

How has *Call Me By Your Name* affected my life? Well, I am just trying to explore this very influence it has had or rather is having as it is definitely not over yet.

"Life has its funny ways" as we all know from the monologue of Elio's father. Sometimes, as I have experienced in my life, love signals in advance that it is coming. I mean a subtle intuition or foreboding that makes you feel that love is coming soon to dominate your life, a kind of impersonal feeling with no specific person related to it.

This was exactly what had swept through my whole being one or two weeks before I started to read André Aciman's book, *Call Me By Your Name*. As there was no potential person in my life, I just did nothing. However, I started to read the book and then watched the film, read the book again, listened to the audio book, watched the film again and again.

I was shocked. Its overwhelming effect, the world started to revolve or rather explode or break into small fragments. The boys moved in my head, brain, and heart. The story chewed me up, swallowed me and spat me out and I had to somehow exist in the meantime.

My work requires quite a lot of mental focusing, oh I suffered, then bought the soundtrack, ringtone and slept less and less. I was in love. I mean, what is this? Walking in the street with eyes full of tears. I had been doing this for a week when I suddenly lost a person I love. To be honest, I was not sure which one was harder to survive, my real broken heart or the fictional one.

I have had a quite hard love trauma, karma or package, whichever I call it. A story I have been carrying for 15 years now. No solution and no way out. I am just so grateful that I am now given the chance to explore through this exceptional piece of art my love story with all the aspects that in this limited human body I am able to explore and slowly and gradually - thanks to my jogging and "Call Me By Your Name music therapy" - find my way back to my soul and peace and the oneness with the universe.

Melinda Wilbur
Budapest
Hungary

I saw *Call Me By Your Name* for the first time on a cold, snowy evening in January of 2018. Watching this film in theaters was a completely transcendent experience. I felt every summer breeze, every ray of sunshine, and every emotion. I had never before been so entranced by a work of fiction - this was a kind of adoration that I didn't know was possible to feel for a film. Although the film to me is a story of love, it is also a story of learning to embrace not only the happiness and joy of life, but the pain and sorrow as well.

I saw in Elio glimpses of my younger self, when I first felt the overwhelming sensation of falling in love with someone I never expected to. I saw in him the ultimatum I too had felt at various stages in my life - the realization that I needed to either speak now or go to my grave, toting a secret of love not fully actualized. He perfectly personified the experience of first love, and ultimately, first heartbreak.

Although every single moment of the film is beautiful, the scene that will always stand out in my mind the most is the conversation that is had between Elio and his father following Oliver's departure. Professor Perlman tells Elio: "We rip out so much of ourselves to be cured of things faster that we go bankrupt by the age of thirty and have less to offer each time we start with someone new. But to make yourself feel nothing so as to not feel anything - what a waste."

Too often in my life I ignored my feelings, or worse - invalidated them. I minimized my feelings to make them seem insignificant, but all I did in the process was make myself feel empty. Pushing away feelings of sadness or loss didn't make those feelings go away - it just made them fester below the surface and come out in unhealthy ways.

The first time I saw *Call Me By Your Name*, I understood the importance of Professor Perlman's words, but they didn't quite sink in. However, during subsequent viewings, his words finally clicked and resonated with me so much that I released tears left over from experiences that had happened years prior.

In the months that have passed since CMBYN first came into my life, I have tried to stop minimizing or invalidating my feelings and emotions, even sorrow and grief, and instead have embraced them. As Professor Perlman says, "our hearts and our bodies are given to us only once."

I will forever be grateful for this beautiful film and the way that it has changed my life. I can't wait to rediscover it in the coming years, and be transported back not only to the winter of 2018, but also to the summer of 1983.

Tricia Stansberry
Columbus, OH
USA

Hello my friends! I have a very different story to tell all of you, for the simple reason that besides living in Crema, I am the vice president of the Pro Loco tourist office of the city and the Facebook page administrator. We manage the tourist boom linked to the film. Starting in January, we received thousands of emails and messages with requests from around the world asking how to get information about the locations in *Call Me By Your Name* and how to visit them. Many told me their stories and how this film has changed their lives.

To satisfy them, we have recreated the set of the film in the station square with bicycles and original chairs (which will remain open until late autumn), printed more than 10,000 leaflets and postcards with as many paths to follow in both Italian and English. They were quickly depleted!

Our office receives fans every day who want to visit the city and dine in restaurants and go to fun places where was the crew did. Let's not forget that Luca Guadagnino lives in Crema and you might meet him at a bar or somewhere around the city!

The curious thing about me is that it took me three months to read the book by André Aciman. I expect it will be a busy summer with many fans visiting the city and other places where *Call Me By Your Name* was filmed. The station square is a popular place for photographs and selfies. We have had so many interesting tourists, including a Danish guy who arrived alone in town dressed as Elio!

Greetings to all and see you in Crema!

Franco Bianchessi
Crema
Italy

I was on Facebook one day in January, and a friend of my daughter posted a status: "Everyone should see *Call Me By Your Name*." I had heard the Oscar buzz surrounding young actor Timothée Chalamet and also vaguely knew what the story was about, and so added it to my list of must-see movies. I work in a local hotel and do not make a lot of money, so I couldn't afford to see it in the theater, in fact I never have had the privilege of watching it in on a big screen. Truth be told, this being small town in West Virginia, *Call Me By Your Name* did not play very long here. Quite a shame, but this is a very conservative state.

I have Xfinity cable, and the day *Call Me By Your Name* became available on On Demand, I didn't just rent it, I purchased it. Boy am I glad I did, because now I can watch it whenever I want to or need to. I am glad I watched it by myself that night, which was February 28th, 2018.

My first thought was, "Look at the gorgeous scenery! I would love to see Northern Italy!" I think the "piano/Bach rendition" scene, is when I fell for the two lead characters. To say that I became emotional would be an understatement. In my opinion, it's not if you will cry- it's when you will cry and how many times.

After the movie was over that night, after I cried into that fireplace with Elio, I watched the movie a second time. I do not think I've ever done that before. That night, the next day, and for many days after, I couldn't get this movie out of my head. I couldn't get Oliver and Elio out of my head. I ordered the book *Call Me By Your Name* by André Aciman from Amazon. For me, an avid reader, it is usually the other way around. If the movie made me cry and broke my heart, the book destroyed me. After reading the last line in the book, I tossed the book across the couch and ugly cried for at least an hour.

I've lost count of how many times I've seen the movie (It's over 50 times) but I have only read the book once, so far. I will read it again; I'm just not ready yet. This story, and Oliver and Elio, have changed my life. The experience of *Call Me By Your Name* has changed me. It's made me want to be a better person; heck, it has made me a better person already. I don't want to waste time, which is so precious. I don't want to waste my life, which is "only given once." I feel a freedom I haven't felt since I was much younger, and I want to live my life without fear, as myself, as I truly am. None of my friends seem to understand how much this story has meant to me, how it affects me so profoundly, how it has changed me. I was looking around on Facebook and so luckily found the *Call Me By Your Name Global Facebook Group.*

My grown-up daughters have not yet seen the movie. But they can see how it has affected me. I came out to them as bisexual soon after the first time I watched it. Both of them were delighted I finally told them; both of them said they already knew, had always known, and wondered if I would ever tell them.

71

My hope is that someday I can visit Northern Italy myself, and see the places where the movie was filmed. I hope I can live my life as a better person who is true to herself as she really is. The great thing is, I hope. For a long time I was simply existing. Now I really want to live. I hope I haven't wasted too much time and can really do that authentically. So grateful I found that Facebook group, and proudly call myself one of the "peaches".

Karen Corona Merritt
Morgantown, WV
USA

I've never had a favorite film. There are films I've loved. Films I've seen numerous times in cinemas. Films I own that I've watched over and over. I could probably tell you my favorite western. Or my favorite horror film. But ONE? I could never narrow it down.

What an amazing character André Aciman created in Elio. It's impossible not to relate to him. Especially if you've ever been a 17-year-old boy. In my case, being gay and a musician as well, I can particularly relate. Elio mirrored so many feelings, experiences, and conflicts I'd experienced throughout my life. But he also showed me things I'd never seen: the way he looks at Oliver immediately prior to the "last kiss in Bergamo" comes to mind. I'd honestly never seen one human being look at another like that. It was breathtaking ...almost otherworldly.

In drama school, they teach us that the goal is complete invisibility of performer and complete transparency of performance. Timothée Chalamet is a revelation as Elio. No matter how hard I study his performance, I cannot find a single false moment or lapse of that transparency. Not one. I've seen a lot of film, theatre, and television, and a lot of fine performances by some wonderful actors. But I've never seen anything this transcendent.

With the first notes of *Hallelujah Junction* and the first glimpses of that gorgeous Italian villa, Luca Guadagnino pulled me in. The gauzy, languid feel. Those snapshots of moments. The music. I was instantly transported and transfixed. There was nothing gratuitous. Nothing disquieting. There was no antagonist. Just beauty and emotion.

So now I can finally narrow it down - *Call Me By Your Name* is, unquestionably, my favorite film of all time.

Mick August
New Jersey
USA

This wonderful, beautiful book. People all over the world fell in love with the setting, and most importantly, the characters. When the movie came out, my love for it became bigger, more passionate. It spoke to my soul, just as the book did. I have never had luck with love or relationships, so to read and see a love like Elio and Oliver's made me cry and wish the best for them.

To this day, I wish they could still be happy together. I see so much of myself in both of them that it hurts to think about it sometimes. We all want love as pure as theirs. I would feel like I was in heaven on earth every day. I've made friends through this book, film, and group.

This has made me feel that even someone like me, who never has luck in love with either sex has a shot in having a beautiful story of my own. To be loved for who I am and seen as something more than a storm of emotions. I want to call someone by my name and be called theirs. To see the world and fall in love with a beautiful person and have an extraordinary life.

I love this Facebook group like family. I hope we all can get together one day and have a wonderful time in Crema together.

Jade Groves
Hinesville, GA
USA

Life is funny. And shamelessly cruel.

I am a scientist by day, an artist by night and a New Yorker at heart. In 2017, I couldn't make my trip to New York City and was feeling such a strong attraction to the city that I haven't felt before. Finally, in the beginning of 2018, I could make my 13th trip to my favorite city. As it was the next day of the bomb cyclone, several of my well-wishers told me to postpone my trip. My friends did not. They know me too well. They know my obsession with NYC.

As the flight was leaving Dallas, I wrote -

"Let it be the bomb cyclone, let it be the cold

New York always welcomes me with a heart of gold!"

Who knew within a day of reaching NYC, something so unexpected, something so emotionally turbulent would happen to me, that I would try to prepone my return ticket to get back home!

So how did it happen?

It was 18 degrees F and it was snowing. I was feeling irritated as I couldn't go see my Angel of Bethesda in Central Park. I was just standing in front of the Plaza hotel and trying to find a place, any place to warm up a little bit. Then I saw a blue colored poster of a film where it looked like a man is resting his head on another man's shoulder. *Rolling Stone* gave it four stars. I crossed 58th Street and walked to the Paris theatre where the film was playing.

I am very skeptical about LGBTQ+ films as most of them are crappy, titillating and they sabotage the art of film-making in so many ways I couldn't even count. Instead of breaking rules, they get stuck in a stereotype. This film, as I read in the review, is based in sun-drenched Italy. It sounded like a pretty good film to watch while warming up a bit inside the theatre.

Little did I know, this film named *Call Me By Your Name* by Luca Guadagnino, would find a tiny opening in my skeptical mind and would plunge a white-hot iron bar through my heart!

I didn't really cry. At least not the first time I saw it. I knew I saw something beautiful, poetic, moving, real, brave, acute, tender and humane.

I moved on with my usual New York City chores: eating Indian food at the Curry Hill, watching the sunset behind the southern tip of Manhattan from DUMBO, meeting my friends and family all around the city, visiting the European sculpture court at MET, the Leslie-Lohman museum in SoHo, so and so forth. But, throughout the day, I felt like going back to the Paris theatre and watching the film again. As if something I had missed, as if something more I was wanting to get out of it.

The second time I saw the film, I bawled so badly! Thankfully the theatre during the day was very empty. I came out of the theatre and started walking across the 5th Ave. I couldn't see the streets clearly as my eyes wouldn't stop watering. And my teardrops would not turn into ice, even though it was 20 degrees.

Suddenly, I could remember all the pain from all my past romantic relationships. Pain that I've frozen away in the form of stalactites in such obscure and faraway caves over the years, that even I couldn't remember they existed. All of a sudden, they all were melting and flooding through my heart, shaking me and questioning the very fabric of reality I built within and around my life. It was not soothing water that put out the fire. It was a scorching lava that reinvigorated the fire.

Then I saw it again. And again. And again. The film was pulling me like it wouldn't let me breathe until I go through all of my own agony.

There are three unique things in this film that moved me:

First, the cinematography, the acting, the sound - made it so natural that I felt I was a character, an observer, inside the film. I could smell the basil in their food. I could taste the apricot juice they were drinking. I could feel the fabric of their clothes as they were cycling by the meadow

75

or swimming in the trough. There were moments where I wanted to reach out and interact with the characters, specifically to guide Elio as he was so young and tender, wearing his heart on his sleeve, very much like me. I read later - this is the specialty of Luca Guadagnino's films.

Second, there is no antagonist that we see here. Neither internal, nor external. Everyone is very supportive of the love the main characters share with each other. I think this point made the separation even more painful. Who should we blame? Elio for falling in love? Professor P. and Mrs. P. for not stopping him? Oliver for not telling that he might get engaged and married to someone else? I tried so hard to be angry and blame someone so that I could turn my own pain into anger and revenge! The way I did in my scientific research by killing cancer cells with novel therapeutic strategies and making discoveries that people appreciated! But, in this case, I just couldn't!

Third, there is a very strong sense of vulnerability that the characters portray - the kind of vulnerability that can only be felt by people young-at-heart. It is brutal, naked yet brave and elating. There is no hero going through the monomythic "hero's journey" described by Joseph Campbell and loved and celebrated by Hollywood! There is no one wearing prosthetics loved by Academy Awards juries.

I was in such an emotionally turbulent state of mind, I wrote to my filmmaker friend in Dallas. She very kindly kept the conversation going until I could turn my pain into something creative.

I thought about a series of abstract paintings. But, I knew immediately it won't be able to capture the plethora of emotions I felt. Next, I thought, I would write the story from Oliver's perspective that the film or the book do not portray. Again, I felt like that wouldn't be satisfactory and fair to the fire I felt in my heart. Then, suddenly, as the 6 train reached the 14 St station, and I tried to keep my balance in the crowded subway, it came to me. I need to make something that combines words and images. I need to make a graphic novel.

76

This creative need was so strong, I immediately wanted to get back to my writing and drawing studio in Dallas. I listened to the 7-hour long audio book of the same name written by André Aciman, on which the movie was based. During the flight, I read the script by James Ivory and started brainstorming ideas about expansion and picked up clues on the protagonist of my graphic novel.

After I was back to my apartment in Dallas, I started writing the script. It took me 15 hours to write 22 scenes of the story that I wanted to tell.

The irony of this experience was that New York City, the source of my strongest obsession, tricked me into experiencing something that broke that very obsession and replaced it with just love.

I don't know enough to understand why the film didn't receive the Golden Globe even with three nominations. I did wish the film won the Academy Award because a genuine story of love combining both joy and pain is highly timely to keep us human even with the lack of empathetic leaders all around the world.

I started to realize that while going through the usual stress, anxiety and pain of life, I have been losing bits and pieces of my heart. As a result, I was also losing the ability to empathize, to feel genuine happiness and was gravitating towards thrills.

Watching *Call Me By Your Name* brought back the pain, the vulnerability, the empathy and the happiness in memories that I've locked down in such faraway places that even I couldn't remember. Now I realize that pain completes the happiness and is essential to be and stay human just like beauty in my art and in my science is incomplete without the suffering.

In the end, I want to steal Sufjan Stevens' words, the hauntingly beautiful songs he wrote for this film, as he said it in a way I never could:

"I've loved you for the last time

Is it a video? Is it a video?"

Dhru Deb
Dallas, TX
USA

Call Me By Your Name caught my heart through the warmth, wisdom and harmony shared. Mr Perlman is both a wise parent and a loyal friend. The way he explains the value of Elio and Oliver's relationship stands out and Elio's tears, in the last scene, heal both him and me. I agree with Oliver: Elio is fortunate to have such a father, a role model for other parents.

I was impressed by the candid and supportive approach in which Elio's father admits to envying his son's unique relationship to Oliver, and inspired by the exceptional way of suggesting that Elio does not let it just slip away. Mr. Perlman clearly illustrates the consequences of having to leave a relationship behind and, above all, the much too common choice among us to "make yourself feel nothing, so as to not feel anything". He recognizes Elio's love, sorrow and pain and advices Elio not to "kill it, and with it the joy."

I identify with both Elio and Oliver, as when I was a young adult I had to leave a country on the other side of the Atlantic. I left four years of teenage love and friendship behind. I cried as much and for similar reasons as Elio. I wish that I, at the time, had someone like Elio's father to support and advise me.

To me, the importance of *Call Me By Your Name* was the healing process within myself, and the inspiration to be a wiser, more compassionate parent and loyal friend to my daughters.

Anna Pärondal
Askim
Sweden

"The world is changed because you are made of ivory and gold. The curves of your lips rewrite history…''

How very true of Mr. Wilde's saying as 'My world' is changed and is being kept changing by stories which are made of ivory, gold and beauty and of course the curves of the boys' lips rewrite my history along with so many others!

It's just a story. Just a group of assembled words and a series of images. How can some combination of letters or a sequence of footage immensely affect someone's mind, messing with the feelings? No surprise. It happens all the time when our souls are on the same wavelength with the whispers of the story itself. Dorian Gray was poisoned by a book. Same here. Only difference is that my intoxication derives from aesthetics, positiveness and sweet perfume of the warmest summer nostalgia.

Here we go. (again!)

It's 1983.

It's "Somewhere'' in Northern Italy".

Six weeks. There is no before but after.

The days are scorching under the Mediterranean Sun, as sweat coming through all over my skin, God, I'm so desperate for a splash of freshness to feel. Let me rest under those trees! They smell delicious. Everything seems delicious here. The sky, grass, the sound of the summer breeze, the blue window shades, the bicycles, those vintage garden chairs… everything you can imagine is bursting with raw beauty. Well, it figures, I am standing on the land of ancient gods; Venus' light has the ability to reach everywhere. Even stones shine dazzlingly! The texture of the fruit under my fingers… How very appetizing! It's no surprise you could easily fall in love with someone who can whisper tempting lullabies into your ears. And the sound of that poignant guitar!

Scuso Elio, troppo rumore; the church bell, horns, people talking, I cannot hear you.

Okay, fun is fun, now it's time to say goodbye to the sweetest dream. Wake up, it's just an illusion, said the voice and kept talking. You go to the work, you go to your school, live your life. Endure the daily problems. Life is running, you need to catch up! Work, study, do more work and study more.

But why?

Do I have to stop living and running after it?

I may be "cursed" by the speed but I can be the life itself! Weren't you my witness last night? I was time! I was 'the moments' the life exists within. I was the script!

It is true that time flies, but I can capture those moments. I can feel them behind my eyes, inside my skull. It's true that time is vicious, but I can make fun of it when I let myself drift through the stories swarming with energy and beauty.

My ability to place myself anywhere, anytime defeats the power of time over me. I'm the eyes that catch the combinations of letters, the catcher of thoughts and feelings. Such a wonderful transaction between the author and the reader! I allow him to use and confuse me with his bittersweet lines. I own everything that he writes.

Then, the moviemaker comes and digs those sentences out of me. He is a sculptor, reshapes everything belongs to me. Change. 'The only thing that is constant is change'. And action! Casting, rehearsal, production, distribution and kaboom! There they are! Elio, I can feel you, deeply, as yours is our story! Conflict is the nectar of life! You're waiting for a smile impatiently, you're being the detective to solve the mystery of those shorts, the way you react when he touches your shoulder. Man, you are me, I am you! We are united by our hearts! And Oliver... How someone can blame you to follow what you feel as we are bound to those delicate moments as we, human beings, are just 'moments in time as we are cursed to be lost in it.' Anyway, can't you hear? Is it your song? Let's dance!

Keep dancing, until the Earth spins, till the universe exists! We'll be forever as we feel the feelings forever!

From my heart to all the creators of this splendid, touching beauty,

Thank you all!

Ozlem Senturk
Istanbul
Turke

Call Me By Your Name has been a blessing for many people of different backgrounds and sexual orientations. As one of many straight people in the *Call Me By Your Name Global* group, we were asked why this gay movie affects us so deeply. My answer always is that I don't see it as a gay story, but a love story.

I have gone through and experienced everything that Elio and Oliver been through: first love, first heartbreak, anxiety about whether to speak or not, falling for someone on a short trip and feeling torn when it's time to return home and also giving someone false hope by giving them attention knowing well that it's forbidden and that I cannot give them my all or my heart.

This nostalgic atmospheric beautiful movie has tapped into our senses, aroused buried feelings and it's very refreshing to share it with others who has also been affected by it. We've made new friends and family, learned about other cultures, inspired by each other's love stories, got recommendations for other books and movies and looking forward to meeting each other in the future.

My personal favorite is the relationship I now have with my Filipino "son" that I met through the group. His mother passed years ago, and I do not have a son so it's music to our ears when we call each other mom and son. Even though we are on the opposite ends of the globe, we check in with each to make sure everything is good and that we are safely at home.

I know this movie inspired some people to come out of the closet, but it has inspired me to be more accepting, open-minded and definitely it has made me more sentimental. I just want to walk up to strangers and hug them tightly.

Donna Marie

In my country they don't admit this kind of love and it's illegal. Even the film is not coming out in our cinema. So in this kind of country I came out when I was a teenage boy. The words, the bullying, the memories. It really, really hurt me. But when I see this film it makes me strong. I still believe everyone deserves a love story that makes you never forget.

Morris

If I'd have known about *Call Me By Your Name* sooner, and how incredible a catalyst it was going to be for change in my life, I'd have bought out my local indie theater the moment they released it. Knowing little to nothing going in, I was immediately welcomed "somewhere in northern Italy" in the summer of 1983 with an enthralling piano opening, a hot, lazy afternoon, and the warmest company I didn't know I needed. Over the following month and two, more viewings with friends who were as equally moved as I was, I fell into the best and worst state of flux of my life.

Battling alcoholism, anxiety, depression, regret and whatever the hell else was wrong with me, it didn't take long to realize this incredible piece of work meant something powerful to me. For two and a half hours, this film let me live vicariously a life that allowed me to confront myself, my demons, and my survival.

It will forever have one of the most special places in my heart. I have developed a deeper love for piano, found great new music, I'm healthier and happier than ever, and look forward to one day visiting Crema and the villa.

Thank you, Luca, Armie, Timmy, Amira, Michael, Esther, André, and everyone else involved, for the love, laughter, colors, music, tears, pain, heartbreak, hope and warmth. And peaches.

I am a better person because of this beautiful film.

Gordon S.
Athens, GA
USA

I don´t know where to start. I was never a person to judge. The only prejudices I have are towards myself, not towards others. Nor I am going to lie and say that I am an open-minded person. I don´t know, I never thought about homosexuality or bisexuality. I never really thought about how these people feel.

When I saw *Call Me By Your Name*, I only saw two people who were falling in love. Honestly, I did not care about the subject of sexuality. It was a beautiful love story. I fell in love with them.

The reality is that after watching the film and especially after reading the book, I needed to talk and exchange opinions with other people who had also seen and read this story. My doubts were enormous about whether I had understood and interpreted well and things that I had not even understood. For this reason, I joined a group on Facebook to discuss this. And to tell you the truth, it was great. It was great because I met many people who identified with this story, many people who also found a place to vent, to tell things that they otherwise would not tell other people.

I am not adept with social networks, but it is this globalization, this type of interaction, what happens through them that I like the most. I like talking about books and movies!

Thanks to this story and to all these people who tell their experiences, their loves and their heartbreak. I can put myself in their place and not live it as something alien. I can see that love simply feels, that we do not choose who we fall in love with, and that it is something beautiful to happen to whoever happens. Joy and pain are part of love and, even so, it is beautiful.

Sometimes I felt something similar for someone, I do not know if I fell in love with that person. I do not know if I'll ever know ... I think it was something very similar to love, but it did not become so.

At the time I suffered more than I enjoyed it, since he was a man who was in a relationship with another woman. I was just a third person. He lied to me and told me they were not together. When I found out that he lied to me and that he used me, it hurt a lot and I got angry. We were not talking for a few years. But in that period, he tried to contact me, and I rejected him several times, until recently. We talked, and I told him I was not angry, that time helped me overcome it, and it was over. Was it over for him? "I keep going back and forth", he told me. Apparently, he never lied to me and maybe I saw him like that at that moment. Maybe it was my first love, something belated, because it happened to me when I was 25 years old. Before that, all my relationships were platonic.

The point of this story is that, at the time, I was so hurt by the lack of love that I decided to erase it from my life and not feel anything else for someone. Literally, I did not feel anything else for someone. It really is a closed book, but deep down I think I'm afraid of suffering again for someone.

This brings me back to *Call Me By Your Name* and I remember the speech of Elio's father. I should have remembered the happy moments. They were few, but there were and not so extreme.

Now I am 30 years old. I am still young, but I wonder why in all these years I did not allow myself to live with someone. Maybe the right person did not arrive, maybe I did not see him pass, maybe he was always there, and I never realized it. I do not know.

I'm not worried about being alone. I'm not in a hurry to be with someone. I always knew that you have to love yourself, so that someone loves you a little more and I am happy with me, I love myself and I enjoy my time with myself. I do not need to be with someone to feel good. I do not worry about being alone, I worry that I will never fall in love.

Lara
Buenos Aires
Argentina

Since January 2018, I've watched *Call Me By Your Name* seven times in theaters and twice at home. Every time, I'm reminded of "what if" moments I've had with close friends I had romantic feelings for and all the opportunities I've missed. I jokingly call these my "speak or die" moments, but unlike Elio and Oliver (and the prince), I chose to "die" because I was scared of rejection. I left every viewing ugly crying; I was so happy that Elio and Oliver spent such a beautiful time together, but I was devastated that I had never had the courage to speak and have that deeper connection with another human being. I became guarded over the last six years, unwilling to let people in and always keeping an emotional distance from everyone.

I lied to myself that emotions were trivial, but the pure joy and love that Elio and Oliver shared with one another broke down these walls and reminded me of how alive I felt when I was in love with someone. Professor Perlman's words to Elio - "We rip out so much of ourselves to be cured of things faster, that we go bankrupt by the age of thirty and have less to offer each time we start with someone new. But to make yourself feel nothing so as not to feel anything — what a waste!" - spoke directly to me and woke me up from a stupor where I buried my emotions.

85

I began to view the world through the lens of emotion and personal connection, to value the richness and color of feeling and instead of cold black-and-white facts. Strangely enough, I began seeing each individual person with a unique story and loved ones instead of strangers walking by me in the supermarket. The phrase "to speak or die?" ran through my head every day like news tickers on the bottom of the screen, encouraging me to live vivaciously and to make decisions that felt truer to me.

Seeing Elio and Oliver's relationship captured so beautifully on-screen was also so important and empowering as a bisexual woman who has yet to come out. This film captured the sentiment that "love is love" and that no label or prejudice should ever weaken the depth of feeling that we, as people, can feel for one another. Love is love is love is love.

On a different level, *Call Me By Your Name* also revived my interest in art and literary classics. I began to sculpt, paint, and read more in my spare time, something I might not have returned to in many years without this movie.

Without *Call Me By Your Name*, I would still be stumbling day-by-day and lying to myself about the importance of human connection, unable to live freely and with emotion.

I am forever grateful to those who made the movie possible, from André Aciman, Luca Guadagnino, Timotheé Chalamet, Armie Hammer, James Ivory, Peter Spears, to Sayombhu Mukdeeprom, and so many more people. Thank you.

LLL
California
USA

I met "My Oliver" in 1983. He was six years older than me, 6'3", blonde, billowy shirts, so sure of himself. Instant attraction, unbelievable passion, I was hooked. My first real love. We had two seasons together. I was the one who left; I couldn't take his unfaithfulness. No trust, alcohol involved.

Later that week, he called my mom and said, "I will be nice to him from now on" (She didn't know what he was talking about. My mom didn't know about us, or that I was gay) She was angry at him for making her find out this way. He tried and tried to get me back, came to my work crying and begging. Yes, my heart was broken and breaking at the same time, I wanted US. But we unfortunately went our own separate ways.

Five years later, we reconnected by phone. Yes, I called him. He apologized for everything he put me through. I was living in a different state at that time. We talked almost every day and we laughed. And always said "I love you" after every call. I was in heaven just knowing I could talk to him again. And fantasize about what could have been. I was also attached to his Mom and Aunt and we got along great.

So it was hard when I left. They were on my side as to everything that happened. And were angry with him about it. Six months later, I went to visit him at the town where he was living. It was just like day one. We had dinner and we both slept really well in each other's arms that one night. We were naked, and one thing led to another ....mmm ...but we didn't.

I was head over heels once again, as was he. We both knew it would never be like it was, as we both had moved on. We talked for another few years and then it was hard to get a hold of him. His mom had a hard time getting to him as well.

One day in 1991, I had this instant and urgent need to try to talk to him when I awoke. I called his number and a friend answered the phone. She said he was not doing well and they didn't expect him to live the day out. WTF ... My blood ran cold as ice. He was in a semi-coma. I talked to her and his mom and told them how I wished I could be by his side. He didn't want to see anyone. Time was not on our side.

They called me an hour later or so and said he was gone. "My Oliver" was gone. My body was instantly cold and numb. I don't think I will ever get past losing him. I really don't know what took him, but I kind of know. The way he looked when we met that one night. He was hiding something ... I have great dreams about "My Oliver". In my dream, we sit on his front porch and hug and laugh and cry. It's the strangest thing. It's like he's connecting with me every now and then. I'm okay with that. But the next morning, I am a wreck. His smell, his voice, his touch ... just like it is real. I so miss "My Oliver".

I have moved on now (sort of), but he is still a very important part of me. I only have one picture of him. I do have a coat he wore and a book he gave me *Looking for Mr. Right But Will Settle for Mr. Right Away* Ha ha. He signed it "Stay Happy and Well My Love"

He will always be with me and is a part of my soul. This film has taken me to the edge of reliving it all over again. I have cried and cried, and I am thankful for this film for reconnecting me with him again, through the love and loss.

Over the years his aunt passed away and then later his Mom, so now I have no physical connection to him if you will. I'm listening to the audio book now and it is hard, but wonderful to listen to. "My Oliver" had a very similar voice. Thank you, Armie!

Jeffrey Wright
Atlanta, GA
USA

I bought and read *Call Me By Your Name* in 2007 when it first came out. I was in high school and also in the closet at the time. I had just moved to the U. S. in 2005 and barely spoke a word of English. But I knew that I was gay and I was yearning for something, someone who could articulate what I felt at the time and make me feel like I was not the only one.

I had read several coming out, gay teen novels before *Call Me By Your Name* and they were all very nice and touching, but none affected me on a fundamental level like *Call Me By Your Name* did, and still does to this day. I probably read the book ten times since I first bought it. I tossed the original book jacket because it was so dog-eared and worn out.

The first few times that I read the book I was still learning English and could not fully understand André's writing which was complex, profound, and beautiful. But the more I read it, the more I understood the story, the characters, and each time I read it, I found something new.

It is a bottomless treasure chest; every time I reached in, I would find a new shiny gem. And now that I am fluent in English and working as a professional interpreter, I read it because I want to take in André's wisdom when it comes to love and human connection.

My heart still breaks every time I read it, but I can't seem to stop myself. And I've recently realized why: to love someone that deeply is to risk getting hurt that deeply, but to deny yourself that opportunity is a disservice to yourself and to the world, because it always needs more love.

Someday, I want to be able to love a man that much, and as for the rest? I'll let it unfold on its own.

I was extremely nervous when I heard that they were going to do a film adaptation of the book because the story is intensely profound, passionate, and gut-wrenching. I didn't think that the movie would be able to do this beautiful piece of art justice. I was wrong. Not only did the movie manage to capture the hearts of so many people around the world, it also gave the book the notability that was long overdue.

Huy Truong
Houston, TX
USA

More than a magnetic cinematic experience, this masterpiece was in its totality an emotional journey like no other. *Call Me by Your Name* seduced me at first, pulled me in, almost hypnotized me, then it made me fall in love only to eventually rip my heart out. Does it sound familiar to you?

It acts like the lover we've always wished we had, like the one we lost forever. We go from lust to agony to ecstasy to joy and lust again – we literally traverse every possible human emotion. It is that kind of movie which by the end of it will make us feel more humane simply because we got to experience it… to experience love at the highest level, in its simplest form.

Once I was caught in this mirage, there was no turning back. I felt so immersed in the story that I began to feel just as enamored as Elio, longing for reciprocity, recalling my teenage years, reliving the better days, when all grass was green, when rivers welcomed me naked and vulnerable… What astounds me about this work of art is that every scene, every landscape, every word, gesture, character – everything seems to be aligned to the love between Elio and Oliver, serving it well.

Each small element helps build a love so intense and disarming, all-encompassing and fresh, consuming and maddening and really unique. Every line, every tree, every fruit, every musical note that Elio transcribes, summer itself – all bow down to humanity's deepest most enthralling sentiment.

As Timothée Chalamet himself states in an interview, art happens in the eye of the viewer. For me, this is a story about lost love and about allowing yourself to grieve. And I will tell you why this aspect of the story stood out for me.

About one year and a half ago, I lost someone I loved deeply. As they decided to walk away from my life, I found myself grieving, a process which is somewhat ongoing. What I have realized, during this challenging phase of my life, is that we need to make sure we go through our emotions and not past them. I firmly believe that no matter the hardships you've experienced, no matter the severity of the hurting, and regardless of how broken and damaged you are, the triumph is in retaining your ability to feel, despite all the pain you've been through.

The key lies in dealing with your every emotion, bit by bit, as excruciating as the process may be, without becoming cynical or bitter as these won't get you anywhere. Disregarding the quietly deafening sound of your emotions only amplifies the very thing you are trying to escape from: pain. The healing is in the aching. And this is exactly what *Call Me by Your Name* has managed to bring forward, brilliantly captured in the speech of Elio's father. Those words have shuddered every atom of my being. And it was my experience with this movie that allowed me to forgive the one I lost.

But there is another strong reason why this particular story spoke to me and why it will probably go down in the history of cinema. Aside from the magnitude of the story that unfolds and the magnificent scenery, it cryptically manages to rise above labels. For someone who is outspoken about human rights and discrimination of any kind, this movie delivered something I had really longed to see on screen. It aims to tell a universal tale and so it escapes identity politics; in that sense, if you think it's a gay love story because there are two guys falling in love, you're missing the point. This is not a gay movie and it's not an LGBT movie.

What is being depicted on the screen is the inner turmoil of a 17-year old falling in love for the first time. Nowhere in the movie is their sexual orientation specified and that's because it wouldn't serve the story. You are watching a younger version of yourself falling in love, longing, exploring and you reminisce about what could have been, and that is regardless of who you are, your gender, your social background and so on.

The movie also stands out because of the graceful way in which it portrays masculinity. In light of a personal and academic interest in gender studies, I have found that the love between the two young men embodies the possibility to bridge a historical and social gap.

Unlike other on-screen love stories between two men, there is not a single trace of compulsive masculinity or violence. For me, this leaves Elio and Oliver gravitating in a utopic universe, outside any gender norms, with only love and tenderness for each other. There is a closeness that is rare between two men on screen, an intimacy that will leave you in awe and a friendship to celebrate all of our most-treasured friendships.

Moreover, there is no eventual punishment, no bullying or ridicule, no death – all ubiquitous elements in "gay- themed" movies. One moment that stands out in the story is the handshake between the two lovers, as a symbol of peace, friendship, unity, and love – all so much needed amidst today's socio-political unrest.

This is a love story that feels genuine, always in your proximity. In the end, you are the one becoming aligned with this force. Because you have retained your ability to feel, as Elio's father advises him, you are trans-formed. But not before you go through the soul-ripping experience of losing the one you love.

The movie's philosophical, linguistic, artistic as well as erotic tones give the story a bohemian vibe and adorn it with many symbols, as we vibrate alongside Elio and Oliver. Every character becomes an artist, not only contemplating, but delivering this nascent and forgiving love. We listen to piano chords from Bach, we savor nature's ripe fruits, we read 16th century French romance, we swim in the river, we make love and hear the leaves of endless possibilities shuffling outside our window. And of course, we wish it never ended. When was the last time you felt this way about a movie?

This splendid celebration of love will bring you back to life, will remind you why it matters to remain open and vulnerable, and why it is always "better to speak." It will not solve the mystery of love, though. But you will most certainly remember this cinematic feast as one of those expe-riences that has touched you in unique ways.

Gregoria Green
Bucharest
Romania

The first time I saw *Call Me by Your Name*, I was overflowing with emo-tions. At first, I connected my strong reaction to my own experiences of young, passionate summer love in Italy. Later, I considered whether it was the amazing parents in the movie which got me the most. Yet, I felt that there was more to define in the film.

So I saw it again, and again, and again. Suddenly it struck me; it all had to do with INTEGRITY, to be complete as a person! (In Latin "integer" means "whole" or "complete") *Call Me by Your Name* speaks to, and calms, my desire for integrity. I feel in harmony watching this movie!

When Oliver and Elio give themselves to one another, calling the other by their own name, a sense of divine entirety arises; their love is vulnerable, mutual and amazingly beautiful. Also, when Elio's father encourages his son to embrace his full spectrum of emotions - because it's part of being a complete human being - there is room for ALL of Elio in his father's love; this too, is absolute harmony.

In a world where people have integrity, true love can develop. When I had reached the conclusion that the film is about integrity, I felt like I had been healed. For me, integrity is the key to the glorious feeling in *Call Me by Your Name* – and it's also the key to life!   I'm now carrying the movie within me as a glimmering insight into how life should be lived!

Johanna Helje
Göteborg
Sweden

The story and the film has touched and also changed my life on different levels and aspects, I cannot describe it fully in words. I am happily together with my husband for 11 years. He is my Elio and Oliver at the same time and I am truly blessed to share this life with this angel of a man.

Because our world has become so crazy and frightening in the last couple of years, I have become a rather depressed and gloomy person. It was deeply touching and moving to see that glimpse again of everything that is good, true, and beautiful in life.

This summer fairytale of love actually made me a more joyful, optimistic person again. We are going to Crema together this summer on a road trip because of this movie. And also on another note, I started going back to the gym 3x a week because of this movie. I can't explain it; maybe I am trying to channel my inner Armie Hammer/Oliver and grow out of my comfort zone.

Thank you to everyone involved for creating this masterpiece.

JS
Central Europe

Elio is so quietly inquisitive. And emotional in an unapologetic way. Arrogant, too. He's a real go-getter. And at 17, I was none of those things. I would apologize for existing if I could. I never told people how I really felt. I never looked people in the eye. I never did anything or could fully experience others. I was not me, nor am I quite there yet.

Even ten years later, I am just now emerging from the closet. It's been slow. But when I first saw *Call Me By Your Name* in January 2018, it put my life - the past misery, the hopeful future - the kinetic but deeply unsatisfying present - into perspective unlike any other film I have ever seen.

After seeing it five times in theaters (driving over 30 miles each time), I felt like I saw the world through different eyes. This is love. This is emotional fulfillment and satisfaction. Something I have never had. It felt possible for me somehow, like my fire was reignited.

Maybe I could have the courage to go after it like Elio did. Maybe I could have what they had. It was hard to come to terms with this. Because both the book and movie made me see the nature of my relationships with friends and family for what they were. And how, in some cases, they were not worth investing in anymore.

I wanted nothing that reminded me of staying in the closet. And I had to act. Mr. Perlman's acceptance of Elio and his now iconic monologue really broke me. I never had a healthy father figure. And I think being gay only made my need for male companionship and guidance that much more intense. *Call Me By Your Name* is idealistic, but "that's the stuff dreams are made of."

Phoenix R.
Rural Ohio
USA

Saturday, March 3, 2018 is a day that I will never forget. It was a typical Saturday, going to see a movie with my best friend. We had made plans to see a special pre-Academy Award screening of a film we had both been reading about, *Call Me By Your Name*, at the AMC Valley View Theater in Dallas, Texas. Little did I know that by the time I walked out of the theater, the experience of this movie would alter my life unlike any other film that I have ever seen.

I have been completely captivated and mesmerized by this beautiful masterpiece. Suddenly, it occupies my mind and heart on a daily basis. The story resonates so strongly with me on a personal level. I was transported back to a period of time over 25 years earlier to my own first love. The story of Elio and Oliver deeply moves me because it mirrors so much of what I experienced with my first love – the beauty, the joy, the heartache and the tears.

My friend and I both loved the film. Afterward, we had dinner at a small Italian restaurant and couldn't stop talking about the movie. This is one of those rare gems that blended together into the perfect film that touches the heart and soul. Beautifully shot, perfectly cast, with an amazing screenplay by James Ivory, based on the words of André Aciman, and all brought together with the artistry of master director Luca Guadagnino.

Call Me By Your Name has become one of my all-time favorite movies. Thank you, Luca, Mr. Ivory, Mr. Aciman, Armie Hammer, Timothée Chalamet, Michael Stuhlbarg, Amira Casar, Esther Garrel, Vanda

Capriolo, Antonio Rimaldi and company for giving us this beautiful gift of love. You all have my undying love and affection.

Chuck Roland
Dallas, TX
USA

I was living my life as a closeted queer guy who lives in country which LGBTQ is strictly forbidden. I gave up hope of finding love because I was unable to conform and follow a traditional heterosexual life, coupled up with the fact that I grew up in a family with a strong religious background. So, I decided to shut myself in and lived this hollow life for years.

But then, in early January I heard about a film called *Call Me By Your Name* and someone gave me a link to watch it. This film got me falling deeper and deeper, no matter how many times I watched it. I realized that I could relate so much to Elio and Oliver. I admired the way Elio chose to let love in and speak his heart, even though he had to struggle with angst, dilemma, and a very little remaining time.

And I can 100% relate to the way Oliver dropped down his mask and facade, and how he chose to embrace his love even though the end was near and inevitable. I should say that watching *Call Me By Your Name* is an addiction that I never ever want to get over.

Without me knowing, this film tore down every wall that I built before. I started to realize that love is all I need in my life, and there is nothing more liberating than showing your true self to the world. I started to search for *Call Me By Your Name*-related local and worldwide groups, and I'm very happy to find that I have allies. I keep hoping that someday my country will be more accepting to LGBTQ community.

You know, I just came out to my best friend yesterday, and I felt something huge has been lifted off my chest. Maybe I haven't found my love yet, but I believe, when the time comes I will be prepared!

Timotius "Timmy"

Call Me By Your Name made me fall in love with film and life again. I could not be more appreciative of its life-altering impact. I've loved film from an early age, and even then, I knew it affected me intensely. I not only watched film for entertainment, but for character development, cinematography, and even the camera angles. But I hit a plateau over the past few years where all movies and books started to blend together and become uninteresting. That changed when I watched and read *Call Me By Your Name.*

I was completely mesmerized. *Call Me By Your Name* reminded my soul why it was drawn so deeply to art. The creators' decision to enhance the natural sounds, use music as an inner emotional dialogue, and the overall mise-en-scene made me forget CMBYN was a film.

Instead, I felt like I was right there with the characters: I was at the breakfast table, drenched in the sun's rays, surrounded by the smell of the orchard, feeling the water on my skin, watching these two men fall in love even before they knew it. Emotions were pouring off the actors' faces and every frame of film is covered in authenticity and love in its purest form, which finds a home in the viewer's soul. This is brilliant filmmaking, and I expect nothing less now.

But most importantly, *Call Me By Your Name* has changed my outlook on life. The whole text, especially Professor Perlman's speech, metaphorically broke me. I unabashedly felt the whole spectrum of human emotion and I hope always to feel, love, and live life that way.

Noel Hahn
Atlanta, GA
USA

Dear CMBYN Crew,

I went to see *Call Me By Your Name* three days before Christmas. My entire holiday, and much of my life thereafter, was derailed by it. Coming home, in the quiet of night, alone, there was simply no way that I could sleep. I spent that first night weeping, masturbating, and finally, around 4 a.m., yielding to poetry. The film and its meditation on desire opened up a font of creativity in me that was irrepressible. I was alive, almost despairing from feeling so much.

Celibate for five years while healing from a painful breakup, some part of me had given up on wanting. And because the world is a mess anyway, I had begun to think that maybe it was better for me to focus on activism and leave my desiring self behind. But while the advice Mr. Perlman gives Elio at the end of the film made its impact on me, it was really just the prettiness of Elio & Oliver's hunger for - and ravenous enjoyment of one another that shifted things and made me weep old tears that I thought had dried up. Those tears watered my feeling body and, all of a sudden, I wanted again. Really wanted.

I want you to know that I am actively dating again. That I am facing my biggest feelings of discouragement and not letting them stop me. That I have found some balance in my previously harried pace of social justice work that had exhausted me and muted my experience of joy for too long.

I didn't watch the news for three months - a break from the harshness of the world that my tender heart required - and I don't regret it one bit. Everything about my life now if softer, slower, more pierced through with beauty.

Thank you. A million times, thank you.

98

want to express my gratitude for this movie, this book, this group
he universe for helping me find the courage and strength to go on
1 it felt like the end of one's world.

1 Xuan Yo
2i
van

ce childhood, I always knew I liked both sexes (especially men), but
ne time I could not define it. In my family things were very open, so
ways said what I thought. In 2009, my father gave me the book *Call
By Your Name* in English. I always liked to read. But I never under-
od exactly why I received it. The book was nice, but was difficult to
lerstand because I was only 12 years old.

couple of years later, my dad died. I had forgotten the book when I
oved and I did not take it.

lite a while after, I accidentally found out that there would be a movie
Call Me By Your Name and I prepared to read it again. At that time, I
as having problems with my boyfriend (yes, I was already "out of the
oset") and I will not say that I identified with the characters, but it made
e feel that love is true.

ly ex-boyfriend (from Russia) was 28 and I was 18, so I thought it
ould be a good idea for him to read it, but he never did. Later, he
onfessed that while I was waiting for someone (or maybe something)
ke that book, he had sex when he wanted: "My soul is yours and my
ody is for them. " That tore me apart. I was very depressed since this
moment.

When I was at the movie's premiere in Mexico and I realized that by
then, that day, I was one year away from finishing with my ex and I still
cried. That made me feel bad. So I saw the dialogue between Elio and
his father and I cried again, but I knew it was true and I felt free.

Last spring, I met a bisexual guy through work and I guess we clicked right away. He came on to me first by asking me out alone and things started to heat up.

We hung out for the duration of the whole summer and I guess he just wanted to play with my feelings. He suddenly disappeared and later admitted to having started with a girl while I was still very much in love with him. I couldn't sleep/walk/eat/work for two weeks. All I could do was imagine him being intimate with that girl, while I was dying in my own deathbed.

Desperate to "win him back", I begged to have a private chat with him after things fell apart. Not only was he reluctant at first, he also appeared unimpressed by my heartfelt confessions to him about how I'd been in love with him all this time. He just insisted on driving me home when I said I was going to walk home in the pouring rain after our midnight talk had become futile. He watched me shut the door to his car and didn't say a word.

When my own mother found out, she asked me why I was doing all this to myself, while the guy was probably somewhere else enjoying his care-free life and couldn't care less about how I was suffering. She said whatever pain I was going through, she had it ten times worse watching her son being trashed like this.

That's when I realized by torturing myself I was also hurting people who loved me more than I could love myself.

In an attempt to find closure, I asked the guy out to watch *Call Me By Your Name* again with me after months of being complete strangers. After the movie, he left the theater calling his then new girlfriend for a long chat while I was shoved aside, and later told me he couldn't imagine how he's ever going to convince his future wife to accept a son like Elio. That's when I realized this one's a complete lost cause.

Now I've moved on and don't think about the aforementioned douche anymore.

I just want to express my gratitude for this movie, this book, this group and the universe for helping me find the courage and strength to go on when it felt like the end of one's world.

Xuan Xuan Yo
Tapei
Taiwan

Since childhood, I always knew I liked both sexes (especially men), but at the time I could not define it. In my family things were very open, so I always said what I thought. In 2009, my father gave me the book *Call Me By Your Name* in English. I always liked to read. But I never understood exactly why I received it. The book was nice, but was difficult to understand because I was only 12 years old.

A couple of years later, my dad died. I had forgotten the book when I moved and I did not take it.

Quite a while after, I accidentally found out that there would be a movie of *Call Me By Your Name* and I prepared to read it again. At that time, I was having problems with my boyfriend (yes, I was already "out of the closet") and I will not say that I identified with the characters, but it made me feel that love is true.

My ex-boyfriend (from Russia) was 28 and I was 18, so I thought it would be a good idea for him to read it, but he never did. Later, he confessed that while I was waiting for someone (or maybe something) like that book, he had sex when he wanted: "My soul is yours and my body is for them. " That tore me apart. I was very depressed since this moment.

When I was at the movie's premiere in Mexico and I realized that by then, that day, I was one year away from finishing with my ex and I still cried. That made me feel bad. So I saw the dialogue between Elio and his father and I cried again, but I knew it was true and I felt free.

When I got home and told my mother, she replied: "You never under-stood that your father gave you that book because he was also bisexual?" And then I understood a lot of things.

I feel very happy and now it's a very important in my life.

M. Antonio Diez Madrid Armenta
Nezahualcóyotl
Mexico

Call Me By Your Name is my story. I was Elio. I was a seventeen-year-old man in 1983. I knew I was gay, but denied the fact. I became Oliver. I had many one-night stands, but didn't want to admit my sexuality.

I got married and had two sons. Not until ten years after my divorce did I accept myself for the gay man that I am. Now out, I am with a wonder-ful man who loves me, my sons love me for who I am, and am now happy. *Call Me By Your Name* made all of my emotions and feelings become real.

I watched this beautiful movie and wept, not so much for Elio's loss of Oliver, but for my understanding what they were going through. I am truly grateful.

Dean Vitamvas
Fremont, NE
USA

We write, it seems, to reach out to others. Whether we know them or not doesn't matter. We write to put out into the real world something ex-tremely private within us, to make real what often feels unreal and ever so elusive about ourselves.

-André Aciman

In the weeks after seeing *Call Me By Your Name*, I kept replaying scenes over and over in my head. The first kiss, Prof. Perlman's speech, that never-ending, heart-rending final shot. But the scene I couldn't let go of was the kiss in Bergamo. The look on Elio's face. It's so innocent and pure. I kept thinking it's a look you only give your first love - that openness, that complete giving over of yourself, before you know how badly you can be hurt. I've heard that Luca told Timothée to look at Armie like he never wants to kiss anyone else. But it's also like he believes he never will have to - he'll never have reason to because that love will always be there.

For a while I wasn't sure why that scene gripped me so much. Then I realized that it reminded me of how I felt when I fell in love with my husband. More than reminded. It brought those feelings back into my body, back to when I was the one with that besotted look on my face. Seeing it made all of those feelings rush back. And it hurt, because I don't love my husband anymore, because I know that love can go away. I knew it already, but I couldn't feel the enormity of what I'd lost until that scene brought it back to me. It was like ripping a scab off of a wound not fully healed. I didn't even know that love, that hurt was still there.

But it is an exquisite pain, one I don't want to turn away from. And that is the wonder of this movie. It reveals a part of us that loves without fear, or at least without knowing exactly how much it can hurt. So it hurts, but it also lets you feel that kind of love again, reminds you that it's possible, and that sometimes it's worth the pain.

Anonymous
Chicago, IL
USA

I remember hearing about *Call Me By Your Name* for the first time. It was sometime in November of last year. I saw a photo of an Italian villa, as well as some other photos that I cannot recall, and the title of the film. I thought, "Huh. A cool little Italian indie film. I might see it." And I promptly forgot about it.

Months later, my friend came to me, begging that I come with him to see this film. He kept insisting that I go, so I eventually caved and agreed to go.

Looking back, that was probably one of the best decisions I've ever made. I met up with him and a few other friends on a Friday night, outside an old movie theater downtown. We bought our tickets and sat down in the theater.

The lights dimmed, and as the opening credits began, piano playing and statues popping up on screen, I wasn't quite sure what I was in for. But as the film went on, I found myself more and more in love with everything I was watching. The music, the setting, the characters, the story, the romance. I found it all so real and incredibly beautiful to watch.

And by the end of the film, as Elio stared into the fire, tears rolling down his face, I was sobbing. Without a doubt, this is the most realistic and beautiful love story that I've ever had the pleasure of watching. I left the theater with my friends, still crying, and just couldn't stop. The film touched me on such a deep level that no other film has been able to reach, and I just want to applaud everyone who was involved in making this film for doing that.

Armie, Timothée, Luca, James Ivory, André Aciman, and all the rest of you did such an incredible job. I thank you, from the bottom of my heart, for making a film that I will forever love and cherish. You all should be so proud of what you've done. Thank you.

Ben Mortenson
Salt Lake City, UT
USA

I accidentally came across *Call Me By Your Name* in January. Accidentally and fortunately. When I first watched it, I felt strangely "emptied", in a way. Then, I tried to process the wide range of emotions I felt all at one time - pain, profound melancholy, sorrow, infinite tenderness and something I'm still not able to name properly - and understood that all of them, which seemed to weigh so heavily on my chest, were eventually my liberation.

From what I was before, from the "nothing", as I call it. Because I felt nothing. I was in a period of total dullness, I felt horribly arid, as if my emotions had been shut in a tiny, claustrophobic space and couldn't escape from it.

But *Call Me By Your Name* has been just like a terribly-needed breath after a long apnea. It nurtured me, giving me what I desperately needed. It gave me love: the love that I, as a nearly 22-year-old girl, haven't still experienced, but felt like it was mine. That kind of love which overwhelms you, that unknown, giant force you don't want to deal with, because it's simply frightening. The love which becomes an obsession, something you need to know in order to be consumed and feel finally complete at the same time. That kind of love which exceeds and even eliminates the division of two bodies and two minds up to the point they become just one entity. The love which can't be labelled because it's simply the love between two souls.

I also felt the love which is acceptance and comprehension all in one, which warms you and tries to shelter you, as much as it can. The love of a parent who knows he can't take your pain away, but will be there to sustain you and accept you in any case, whoever you choose to be. That love which doesn't judge, but silently listens.

Love in all its forms, that's what I received. And with it, I also received the most important reminder ever: to always accept and give only this kind of love, not accepting less, not giving less.

Sarah del Grosso
Milan
Italy

108

Watching *Call Me By Your Name* filled me with such melancholy. I have never seen such tenderness between two men depicted in a film. So many gay films feature sex, but few show sweet gestures. The way Oliver rubs his thumb in circles on Elio's hand on the balcony, the playfulness when they "played footsie" that first night, Elio constantly tousling Oliver's hair, the light kisses on necks and cheeks, etc. It was so beautiful, but I felt so sad.

My "Oliver" died 15 years ago. I miss taking showers with him in the morning, spooning on cold nights, cuddling in front of the fireplace. We had our own silly language and nicknames for each other. I have no problem finding a sex partner. What I crave is intimacy. I often wonder if I will find another lover like that.

Anonymous

This film touched me deeply for the simplicity of the characters, the environment, the relationship of the parents and family in general, the relationship of respect and love towards employees. As a babysitter working in New York City for very wealthy families who let their children know how rich they are, I see them entering in a competition for money from an early age. I think that the film focused on relationships in a very beautiful way.

Marjorie Andrewartha
New York, NY
USA

How this beautiful movie touched my heart!!

Dearest Luca, and all the wonderful people who helped you make this masterpiece: xoxo

To be honest, I had not heard of this movie until its Toronto International Film Festival debut and Oscar nomination. It was a cold, snowy winter Sunday in March in Canada when I selected this movie to cuddle up to with a small fire and glass of Pinot Grigio. The moment I hit play, I knew I was going to love this movie: the music, the beautiful photography and the desire to be "Somewhere in Northern Italy"at that very moment.

The film truly floats along with scenery, dialogue, music, wonderful actors and a desire to be back in 1983 with love in our hearts. Every scene is captivating and memorable in the soul, just so simply beautiful and love was never more present in my heart. I was amazed how I was feeling watching this love story come to life. I was immediately drawn in and falling in love with love all over again.

After changes that take place in your own life, this movie reminds you that love is important in life, even when you don't want to feel hurt from it. The moment the movie ended, I was in a bit of a daze and a sensual happy place like I had just been moved by a movie and experience that has never happened before.

I was trying to figure the feeling out, and the only way to describe it was that feeling when you first fall in love and forever want to bottle that beautiful "butterfly in your stomach" feeling all over again. You are then so enchanted and want to watch every scene with more intense desire to see the beauty that first captures you, over and over and over again. You completely fall in love with Elio and Oliver, and the entire family.

This is one of the most truly magnificent movie masterpieces that will forever live within me. Most can never really say that you have such feelings from a movie in their lifetime. Thankfully I was not going crazy alone and watching it over and over to enjoy this love story, the scenery, the music and love and more love.

I found the *Call Me By Your Name Global Facebook Group* going through the same intense emotions and passion for the brilliance Luca brought to the screen and so incredibly affected us all to share and connect with love in our hearts.

I can't honestly tell you how many times I have watched this movie, read the book, and listened to the music CD, but it is and will remain endless. Thank you for sharing your magic and touching my heart. Love is shared. Love hurts. Love brings us together no matter what.

Thank you for letting me fall in love again.

Lesley Dymond
Kitchener, Ontario
Canada

This movie – to me – is an absolute masterpiece in every aspect of its making. It is the most beautiful film I have ever seen in my life, truly. I say this, and I feel it from the bottom of my heart. Watching it and sitting there through the credits hit me hard. The story of Elio and Oliver resonates within me deeply and is heartbreaking and tremendously beautiful beyond everything I have ever seen. It is tender, sweet and very authentic.

I really felt like I was there, with Elio and Oliver, breathing the same air, walking the same places, smelling the peaches, dancing to the music, listening to the cicadas while taking in the warm summer breezes coming through the windows and open balcony doors.

There is the scene between Elio and his father. It just hit me right in the stomach and ripped my heart out. When watching it for the first time I was completely crushed; the words just blew me away. I couldn't help bursting into tears. And when you realize that was not even the end and don't know what the movie still holds there for you, you cannot – at last I couldn't – stop crying.

This movie totally messed me up. But in a good way. And it left such a wonderful bittersweet feeling within me. It was painfully beautiful. Many of its scenes I am sure will resonate in me forever. It touched me deeply, moved me beyond anything I have ever seen. I feel very much for their story and also have the feeling of cleansing something from myself that held me back in my life from being truly who I am emotionally, out of fear of being hurt. It makes me want to live life to the fullest, and be true to myself and my feelings.

I'm so grateful to all involved in this project and how much effort and love they put into it. This experience will stay with me forever. Love and love and love. Always.

Romana Piiroja
Graz
Austria

As a 75-year-old gay man, I thought I had probably seen it all. I've been going to the movies since I was a small child in the 1940s - and that theatre is still there, a beautiful, free-standing building but now in another incarnation.

My two favourite films have been nominated as the best musical ever made and the best western ever made. I loved them long before they were listed, but even they have not had the impact that *Call Me By Your Name* has had. Those films never affected me at all apart from their entertainment value.

This film has stopped me in my tracks. The sheer beauty of the whole production takes my breath away: the direction, the cinematography, the settings, the colour, the eternal story of love, the music, the characters, the intense insight of André Aciman's wisdom about human nature, the various interactions of the characters, but above all, the beauty of the relationship of the two main protagonists and their portrayal by Timothée Chalamet and Armie Hammer.

I once had a love like that, with a similar age difference, over a little longer time period and I too had to leave with no hope of a return. All that came flooding back and with the sadness and regret, an incredible feeling of joy that I had had such a time in my life and here it was being portrayed on screen.

For the last 27 years, it has been my privilege to have an "Elio" in my life. Our age difference is considerably more. As time passes, relationships tend to become stable, staid, part of the daily routine, but this story has renewed us both, refreshed us, made us appreciate again what we have, what we've experienced and how lucky we are that we have been able to stay together. No tragic phone call for us.

Call Me By Your Name made me cry profusely during and over time: it still does when I watch it. It made me burst into tears at inopportune times - like in the supermarket or on a bus or while driving. It made me numb for days, but has made me think and ponder and evaluate and appreciate and marvel that I live in a world where another human can pen such beauty and wisdom and another human can translate that writing into a script and another human can bring it together and produce such beauty and other humans can inhabit the characters that have had an impact on so many people across our truly beautiful globe.

John Lincolne
Brisbane
Australia

So, here's my story of how the movie has touched my life:

It all started when my best friend told me I needed to see a beautiful movie as soon as possible when I visited him for a sleepover. Actually it all can be summarized by "I came, I saw, I loved" because that's exactly how it was with me and the movie.

At the beginning it relaxed me, then it gave me chills, a bit of arousal and fun, but then the ending came, and my life hasn't been the same ever since. As an artist, the movie inspired me to create new art, I met new people thanks to that, discovered new music (especially Sufjan Steven's music) which I'm very grateful for.

I also struggle with severe depression - the actors I love with all my heart, especially Timothée, helped me distract myself from bad thoughts, would always make me smile or laugh. Working on fan art related to *Call Me by Your Name* or checking on the cast on the Internet keeps my mind busy, makes me look forward and relaxes me.

I'm in love with this piece of art to this point I'm actually planning on getting tattoos related to it. I hope one day to meet anyone from the cast or crew and be able to explain how much I'm grateful for this master-piece. I'm recommending this movie to everyone I know, encouraging them and making them fall for it, too. It's like my friend who's always there, helping me and inspiring me every day.

Julia Berg
Poznań
Poland

How did Call Me by Your Name change my life? Well first of all, let me start on how I saw the movie. For three long years, I have been thinking and longing for someone to love me romantically ... and well, it seems that by doing so, it hasn't been healthy for me. So after three years, I decided to just watch LGBT movies, specifically gay movies.

I saw the trailer for Call Me by Your Name. I was intrigued that it was not a typical gay movie. I saw that the main protagonist was a bit younger than his love interest. After two weeks of searching, I was finally able to watch it.

Let me tell you, it made me want to fall in love, but it also scared me. It took me away from the idea of being in love for I was a bit depressed with the idea that no matter how much you love each other, if time and destiny will be against you, it will never be.

The movie broke my heart and I cried for both of the characters, that for the first time it made me feel empathy for them. It made me feel and think of the hurt that they have, of how much it hurt that the person you love will never be with you, even if you guys wanted to.

I have been in love and I see so much of myself in Elio, that he was young in love, scared, doubtful and indecisive, which basically describes me when I fell in love with this guy.

The moment came when I read the book and it made me feel even worse because the fact that Oliver and Elio saw each other and although they both know that they wanted each other, but they couldn't ...

I have realized that the movie stays with you and haunts you for a long time. This movie scarred me for life. It was an unforgettable experience. I loved every bit of it and also have been hurt. It feels that my heart has been shattered and pulverized. It taught me to seize the moment, that if you like someone, go for it. It taught me to value the moments you have with someone, but it also taught me to be strong, that not everyone who was with you will always be there. One day they might leave.

It made me believe that you don't need to identify your gender; if you like someone or love someone no matter straight, gay, lesbian or what-soever, you will still love them. You don't need to address which is which.
Also, there are parents who will never judge or criticize their sons or other people for who they love.
It made me realize a lot of things about family and friends as well as gender, love, and that no matter the religion, love is love.

I am literally crying while typing this. I loved sharing this; it makes me feel a bit better. Spread the love and never cry for things that ended, but smile for those things happened.

Louell Emerenciana
Montalba Ruzal
Philippines

I was having dinner with my boyfriend when I first saw *Call Me By Your Name*. We were celebrating Valentine's Day. He took a 3-hour trip to get to my city to visit me. We went to a fancy restaurant and we decided to go see a movie at the last minute. I told him there was this little film that was being praised by the critics, but we had no idea it was about two guys falling in love.

We went inside and when it started I was surprised because I had no idea Armie Hammer was in the movie. Minute by minute, scene by scene, line by line, I started to fall in love with Elio and Oliver and every single detail the movie had.

It was the part where Elio's nose starts to bleed and then Oliver takes care of him. He kisses his foot. It was then when my heart broke in two. I realized I had been Elio in my relationship and my boyfriend was my Oliver. I had never related so much to a character like I did with Elio. I immediately wanted to know everything about Timothée Chalamet and read the book.

The part where Elio and Oliver have sex for the first time was everything to me. My boyfriend liked it too, but he wasn't feeling it the way I was. That scene is so well done, magical, sensual and delicate that it made me even more sad.

My boyfriend asked me why I was crying and all I could do was cry even more. All I wanted to do was hug Elio and tell him it was okay. I've been through this, not being able to be with the love of your life. Luckily, we figured things out and now I get to be. This film helped me realize how lucky I am to be enjoying life with my true love.

André Aciman, thank you so much for writing this story. It touched me, destroyed me, then put me back together in so many ways. Luca Guadagnino, James Ivory, Timothée Chalamet, Armie Hammer, Michael Stuhlbarg, Amira Casar, Esther Garrel, Vanda Capriolo and everyone else involved in the making of the movie, you've done it perfectly.

José Luis Rivera
Monterrey
Mexico

Call Me By Your Name was recommended to me by a former colleague of mine. I used to work as an exhibition curator at a film museum and have therefore seen tons of movies from all decades and genres. None has impressed and affected me as deeply as CMBYN has. I watched it at home, alone. I didn't have any expectations. Afterwards, I felt as dumbstruck as Elio feels during his father's monologue. I sat in my dark living room for about a half hour, feeling, crying, thinking – sad and unbelievably happy at the same time, unable to believe what I had just seen. I'm glad I was alone then, as it was such a personal experience.

This was three months ago. Since then, I have watched the movie seven times – at the cinema, open-air, at home again, alone, with my husband, with friends. I have read the novel and listened to the audiobook several times. I listen to the soundtrack every day (up to the point that my two little kids start singing along). I consume everything I can find about it online, and have put up posters (I have never before put up posters of anything, actor, movie, or band).

I was very surprised and relieved to find out the I am by far not the only one reacting to *Call Me By Your Name* in that way. I haven't quite figured out yet why this movie resonates with me so deeply. I just love, worship (!) every minute of it, the colours, the atmosphere, every line of dialogue, all the silent moments and the ones filled with music. Oh, the music! And oh, those actors, oh, the chemistry!

To me, it's a perfect masterpiece that just gets more and more beautiful every time I watch it. I respond to *Call Me By Your Name* not only on an emotional level, but also on an analytical one, finding pleasure in closely deconstructing how the movie achieves its effects.

Luckily, my husband is not only very patient with me, but being a filmmaker himself, appreciates learning more about the way CMBYN is so full of detail, about its style of cutting, about its narrative approach (especially how it transfers Elio's point of view from book to film), about how it creates its unique visual poetry.

I know some people feel rather devastated by it, but to me the movie conveys a very positive, life-affirming feeling. CMBYN has inspired me to resume my piano playing, which I gave up ages ago. It has deepened my emotional responses to people, to friendship, to music, to poetry, even to the sun (and to peaches, of course) – to life, in general. The movie, or rather the experience of the movie, feels like a treasure that I will carry around with me for the rest of my life.

Anonymous
Cologne
Germany

Call Me By Your Name loosened emotions I haven't felt in years, in decades. I'm straight, old enough to be Armie's mother and Timmy's grandmother. I have seen the movie only once and read the book in the past three weeks, but can't get away from it. It seems to have taken up a permanent space in my head. Why? Because of the tenderly erotic love scenes? Because it reminds me of paths not taken with lovers and friends when I was younger? Because I wish I could have been more like the Perlman's in raising my son? Yes, and certainly because the movie made me feel more empathy for what my younger and older gay friends have gone through to reach the places they are in life, in relationships and in marriage.

I was widowed suddenly a few years ago; my husband was the love of my life. We traveled widely in Italy as newlyweds, and I can't shake those scenes of the countryside that mesh with scenes I remember from thirty years ago. But even if I hadn't traveled in Italy then, I know the movie would have shaken my feelings about love, hope, family and mourning.

Since my husband's death, I've rebuilt my life with many friends and activities that matter to me. *Call Me By Your Name* kicked me out a comfort zone I'd come to rely on and made me again realize what the loss of those previous loves mean now.

The movie has also offered some welcome relief from the political outrages here in the USA. I'm a political junkie, but becoming engrossed with CMBYN has provided an emotional and mental escape from all the outrage on Twitter and Facebook.

I've watched a lot of the *Call Me By Your Name* post-Oscar videos, and it seems that Timmy and Armie and the other cast members have moved on, but I/we can't. Will I? Do I want to? I'll be waiting for the sequel to find out, despite knowing that Aciman doesn't like definitive endings.

Anonymous88
Chicago, IL
USA

I come from a religious family and homosexuality is not talked about.

Starting in my adolescence, I felt this attraction for the men's bodies, especially men's calves. I tried to be inconspicuous and not reveal this.

I grew up unable to control this attraction. I had good classmates with

whom I became more intimate and we discovered this kind of love by sharing common pleasures.

Then came the time when everyone around us wonders "When is he going to get married and start a family?" There was such social pressure from everywhere. So, I got married, started a family, and later become a grandpa. But deep inside of me remains this attraction.

Then one day at my place of work comes a handsome man younger than me. He worked right next to me and little by little our relationship as colleagues transformed into a friendship, where we tell each other our pasts, our loves and disillusions. I was there for him and suddenly out of nowhere, from the bottom of my heart, I felt this desire that I no longer wanted to repress my feelings for him.

How to do it? Do I tell him, and risk losing that companionship or shut up and continue to be his colleague? I chose to write to him what I felt for him. In return, he made me understand that he appreciated my feelings and that my presence was sweet and pleasant. But he simply told me "You are married, and you have a family. I do not want to kiss you, even if I have to suffer because of it."

My heart broke, but I accepted that, preferring to keep this angel to myself and not to lose him. So that was our choice.

Then one day he lost his job where we worked and it all became dark for me. Not to see his smile anymore, to share those moments of happiness, the simple strokes of our hands. We only had meetings from time to time and occasional phone calls.

Then came the day I saw *Call Me By Your Name*. This wonderful film gave me the strength to come back to life. After seeing the movie, I called him and asked him if he saw the movie. He said no and that he would like to see it, but not alone. I jumped to this occasion and offered to accompany him.

We sat next to each other and suddenly I felt his hand on mine, his breathing becoming deeper and deeper. Without knowing what's happening, I turned to him and saw tears falling from his beautiful blue eyes. I gently put his head on my shoulder. Then, our lips joined in a kiss full of love, so natural, so unrestrained. The rest is a little complicated, but we are both confident ....

M. A. D. – Edouard

Call me by your name. Call me by your name. It was Oscars night and all I heard was *Call me by your name* this, *Call me by your name* that.

'What a stupid name for a film!' I thought. 'What the fuck does that mean? "Call me by your name?"

Then that kid's smiley face, so arrogant ...With his mom!! Nominated for an Oscar alongside Daniel Day-Lewis, greatest actor of all time. The nerve! And they kept saying that he was great. Such a discovery. Me, all I could see was the impertinence that showed in his smart-ass face. Then James Ivory shows up wearing that shirt. What a nuisance. I already hate the kid.

Three Billboards Outside Ebbing, Missouri does not win. My favourite movie, it does not win. Worse than that, *The Shape of Water*, which I absolutely hate, wins. My night is ruined. Oscars are ruined forever. I will never trust them again...

It's next Monday and mom says, "Let's go to the movies and watch that *Call Me By Your Name* thingy." Okay, what else could go wrong? Let's go! I already know it's shit but ...Let's give it a try! Let's prove the fucking Academy wrong again!

And then the next thing I know, this stupid kid has provided me with the best performance I had ever seen. The most touching story I had ever seen. The best two hours of cinema that I will ever get the chance to experience.

I did understand what "Call me by your name" meant. I did see what

honesty and generosity looked like. I recognized innocence and truth hidden behind the arrogant, smiling face. And I knew my life had been changed forever in that precise spot in time and space. So, Timmy, for as long as I live, I will hold that gaze of yours from the other side of the fireplace and call you by my name.

Mariana Jorge Lozano
Arcade
Spain

Call Me By Your Name, like a gift from a benevolent force, from the hearts of the artists that conceived and created it, validated a buried experience and acknowledged the sacredness of a love I had lived 24 years earlier. I cried a river. Yet finally after 24 years, I was healed.

What ensued has been freedom and a celebration of life and rejoicing and gratitude and a renewed thirst for art, for music, for film, for travel. The joy is tremendous. *Call Me By Your Name* is a celebration of the fluidity of love, of unconditional love in all its forms, not just the goodness of a particular faith, but the goodness of faith itself, the force of love of being a parent, the force of love in friendship and the importance and value of feeling our emotions wholeheartedly, experiencing them fully, even the painful ones. It is about letting disarming life experiences in again and again, whenever they are sent to us by Grace, learning to speak, not die lest it be too late.

Alas, too many of us consciously or unconsciously or against our will, choose to die, not to speak of the love we feel or the loves we have felt. *Call Me by Your Name* has resuscitated us back to life and given us the strength to accept ourselves, grieve the loss, celebrate that it happened and FEEL again.

Anonymous

After listening to the Hay Festival replay "André Aciman & Colm Tóibín from Sunday 3 June 2018", it clicked. I have understood the fundamental core of why Aciman's writing speaks to me on such a profound level. It is partly that he has captured a moment of unconditional love in my life and distilled it on paper, acknowledged it and made it valid and timeless for me.

However, It runs far, far deeper than that. André 's background (Egypt, Italy, USA, Jewish etc.) much like mine, which is also mixed and varied, had always left me feeling like a citizen of the world, not just of one nation. I also have always had a strong sense of fluidity and dislike of labels. Having migrated several times throughout one's life, the theme of loss, the question of memory, time, belonging, changefulness and validity of experiences in space and time forever linger.

There are not always the same witnesses, geographic surroundings, cultures, religious practices or languages. It's something that becomes your "normal", because that is all you've ever known. However, it can be a difficult existence due to the sense of dramatic shifts and changes that seem to perpetually take place. Finding the words to describe, to immortalize and stabilize the experience is incredibly difficult.

André, for me, has found the words I could not. He has inadvertently helped me find a way to express and stabilize the conflicting experience of having compartmentalized memories and simultaneous inner lives, parallel lives. Places and things I can never return to that still whisper to me, like the smell of freshly baked bread in the oven.

Somehow with his words, I can now, finally make peace of the inner ever-shifting dynamic worlds. He makes me feel okay about it. And I imagine in today's world with so much displacement due to immigration, it is exactly what we need. A way to find peace with leaving behind anything we have known to be "home" in our lives, which includes a place, a house, a person or a powerfully-lived experience and without disowning the past experiences, or the memories, finding a way to be OK with whatever the "new normal" is, even if it holds the bittersweetness of grief within it. I have so much gratitude for this extraordinary being.

Anonymous

Watching *Call Me By Your Name* was a wake-up call for me. I realized I was not really living, but merely existing. Every morning I wake up, eat my breakfast alone, take the bus to a job that I dislike, take the bus home, eat my dinner alone, go online, and go to sleep. Occasionally I will go out with friends on the weekend. But I have not been in a relationship for years. I have not traveled to foreign countries.

Seeing the beauty of Northern Italy, the delight in dining alfresco with friends, tasting the fresh fruit from the orchards, experiencing the giddiness of love … it occurred to me that I couldn't remember the last time I felt true happiness. I was depressed without realizing that I was depressed.

Life goes by so fast. I thought of my father who died before he collected his first social security payment. He procrastinated and never got to do any of the things that he really wanted to do. I don't want to be like him, so I made my "bucket list".

I have always wanted to travel to France, but don't have a lot of money. I heard about house-swapping, where you live in someone's home while they live in yours. I joined a house-trading website and am in the process of fixing up my home. Next year, I hope to finally make my dream come true. Where there is a will, there's a way!

At last I feel hopeful about my life. It would be nice to have a romance like in the movie. But even if I don't, I will enjoy all the new and different places I will explore and people I will meet. It is so nice to have something to look forward to!

Anonymous
USA

Both the book and the film moved me deeply and made me re-examine my life, especially the idea of "parallel lives". I think about my "what-ifs" constantly, though I know it is not healthy. I wonder if I should have married my first lover. What would my life had been like? I wonder if I should NOT have stayed in a relationship as long as I did.

I wonder what my life would have been like if I had made different career choices, if I had bought the house I really wanted, if I had done things that I truly wished to do instead of always compromising and giving in to what others desired.

What if I had chosen what was in my heart instead of always worrying what others would think? I identify with Oliver because I understand him. In 1983, if I was a college teacher wanting to be a tenured professor, would I have had the courage to have a same-sex younger lover and jeopardize everything? Probably not.

I am trying now to live an authentic life and stop concerning myself with what others think. I realize now that most people are living their own lives and don't even care or notice anyway and that is the most liberating thing of all.

Thank you to all those involved in the making of *Call Me By Your Name*.

Anonymous
New York, NY
USA

When I was in my early 20's, I fell in love for the first time. He was a college professor, twenty years older than me. I had already graduated and was not his student, so there was no abuse of power in the relationship. We had such a strong physical attraction, we could hardly keep our hands off each other. But he would cancel our dates at the last moment and be very secretive.

When I tearfully confessed my love, he admitted that he was married and had a family in the suburbs. The downtown apartment where we met was not his residence; it was only his pied-à-terre. I was so desperate for his love that even though this revelation was upsetting, I still didn't want to let him go. But now that I knew his secret, he broke it off. I remember crying for days, but there was no one I could talk to. I felt suicidal at times. I thought I would never get over it.

But here is the thing: I did get over it. And not only that, I have not thought about it in decades. That is, until I saw *Call Me By Your Name*.

The last scene where Elio is crying at the fireplace could have been me and it brought back all the memories that I had suppressed for 40 years.

I cried for Elio, but I also cried for myself. I wanted to tell the young me, "This too shall pass." And tell it to every person who is going through rough times and may feel suicidal. It may be a cliché, but things will get better, even if you can't imagine it right now.

Anonymous
USA

I cannot stress enough how this book and movie changed my life. It not only touched the deepest parts of my soul, but it also inspired me to continuously fight for equal rights in my country which condemns love.

As a kid, conservative ideas were instilled in me, but as I grew older I began to question the need for these closed-minded opinions. The book bolstered my confidence in fighting for what I believe in and for what is right. And helped me accept myself and others who struggle with finding who they are in this world - how love will and shall prevail.

I would like to thank the cast, producers, and everyone involved in making the film. How you made a difference in my life as well as countless others! And a special and most magnanimous thank you to André Aciman for creating such beauty and for encapsulating love.

I shall end this with my favourite quote by Armie Hammer: "Love is love is love is love!"

Jao Gentiles
Tacloban City
Philippines

"Call me by your name and I'll call you by mine."

Being a girl from Greece - a heavily religious country - has an impact on the way you see things. More correctly, it has an impact on the way things are presented TO you.

Call Me By Your Name came out of nowhere and shocked me down to my core. It started out as a "fun watch" along with friends, friends who made some fun of it, all in good nature. Somehow though, I couldn't be a part of it. And by the end of the film, I was a hot mess. I liked it a lot, but I didn't fully appreciate it or even understand it. A lot of things were lost on me, due to my lack of concentration, but I knew that something was different. I felt a hole that needed to be filled, so I made a note to myself to watch it again while completely alone, which I did the next day. And that's when it happened.

You see, for me at least, there are things in life that have an incredible impact. *Call Me By Your Name* was one of those things. When I watched it again, alone this time, I became Elio. I fully connected with him. I felt his confusion, his feelings growing, even his inevitable compulsion to act childish.

One way or the other, we've all been Elio in our lives, and we've all had our Oliver. What I loved most though, was Elio's courage. It was so refreshing watching someone push away his fears and go after what he truly wants. No shame, no regrets, just full-on sentiment. It was so brave and so inspiring.

And then the pain came. I didn't know how physical pain could be possible, but it was. When Elio whispered "I don't want you to go" while crying, completely vulnerable, I felt my heart being ripped out. I have been him in my life, and the realness of that scene, hit me like a truck. I started bawling my eyes out as it finally occurred to me that this was the beginning of the end.

Then their trip came, and reality finally caught up with them - and us. The train scene was my ultimate low. The way Elio clenched Oliver's shirt, the way they said nothing - because let's be honest, what could have been said? The way Oliver looked at him once he was inside the train, and finally the way Elio broke down when he called his mother, were all too real, too strong and too sad for me to handle. Armie is amazing, but Timothée's acting was exceptional and so successful in ripping my heart out.

Then came the "talk" with Mr. Perlman. The talk reanimated my heart, only for it to be killed again. A ray of hope and an example of what a parent should be. A refreshing change to all the other portrayals of parents in movies. This was the scene that had the biggest impact on me, on my friends, on everyone.

Greece, as I have already mentioned, is a deeply religious country. That being said, homosexuality is still considered an anomaly, and bisexuality barely exists as a concept. Watching a parent react the way Mr. Perlman did, gave hope to me.

I don't think I have the strength to talk about the last scene of the movie. It was something I was certain was going to happen, because let's face it, reality sucks and a happy ending only happens in movies. I respected the writing more because of it, though. It was raw and believable. It was realistic, and it had an impact.

People sometimes argue why Oliver did what he did. They argue whether he truly cared about Elio. They are mad at him. For me, it was as clear as day that Oliver cared for Elio so much that it actually surpassed the depth of Elio's feelings. Elio was a compulsive teenager, who went after what he wanted, while not thinking of the consequences.

On the other hand, Oliver weighed all the factors and tried to control himself. He could have easily given into Elio's "pressures" just to have a good time, without giving much thought to the impact that would have on the teenager. But he didn't. He resisted for as long as he could and then he couldn't anymore. You see, it's all the small things. The looks, the touches, the innuendos.

And then their first night together came and it became painfully clear that Oliver cared for Elio more. Just watch Oliver's face change when Elio gets up from bed the next day. Just watch happiness turn to worry and then turn to realization in a second. Then watch Oliver's concerned face when they decide to go for a swim, and we see them exiting the house. And then his fear that Elio was already sick of him. It was so sad watching him being torn between happiness and self-doubt. Finally, watch Oliver's face, their last night together, while Elio sleeps. Everybody keeps talking about how Elio felt, but for me it was about both.

Elio jumped without thought into this, while Oliver had to win all his inner battles, and cautiously leap into this. And to me, this had a deeper impact for him, than it did for Elio. Once he was in, there wasn't any way out for him. It all became about Elio. And when he left, my heart ached for them both. Elio was left behind with wonderful and understanding parents, while Oliver went back to a life that probably didn't feel as his own. So I don't know who had it worse. I just know that this scene was a punch in my guts, and there isn't a single moment when I think about it, that doesn't make me tear up. And I don't think it ever will be.

Call Me By Your Name is not for everyone. Not everyone will love it. Some might even hate it. Don't be mad at them; they just don't understand it. My best friend doesn't understand why it's one of my favorite movies ever. She tried to, but she can't. And I don't blame her.

Movies tend to leave a different impression on everyone, because they mean something different to everyone. I don't think I will ever forget the way it made me feel when I watched it. The way it still makes me feel, many viewings afterward. The sadness and the clenching of my heart when I think about it and all the ways I related to Elio AND Oliver. So no, it's not for everyone. What is for everyone, is Mr. Perlman's talk. It's an exceptional monologue phenomenally delivered, and it's what love should be.

Elio Perlman is a bisexual teenager, and a ray of hope for me. At a time where homosexuality was taboo and AIDS was plaguing the world, Elio shows us that while others' sexuality was being crippled by society, he decided to stay true to himself.

At a time when you had to hide who you really were, *Call Me By Your Name* showed us the importance of understanding parents and what impact they have on a child's life. How fundamentally different it was for Elio and Oliver to move forward from their summer romance. And eventually how it made me - a bisexual girl from an old-fashioned country feel.

Love is love is love is love and I'm grateful I got to experience that with them. Someday, I may find someone to call me by their name and I'll call them by mine.

Eirini Doura
Athens
Greece

When I first saw *Call Me By Your Name*, I was blown away. It knocked me off my feet. A love story that captured my heart and soul. For years and years, I have struggled with my sexuality. I knew during my teen years that I had feelings not only for males, but females, too.

Coming from a strict Catholic family, there was no way I could ever tell my parents. So I grew up, had two children, and kept this secret. I vowed that I would never let my children feel the way I did.

So after I saw *Call Me By Your Name* I cried, especially when Elio's father was talking to him. I wished my father would have said that to me.

The movie had a big impact on me. I had the courage to let one person know I was bisexual and that was my father. I cried many tears telling him and how watching this movie gave me that push to reveal my sexual preference.

To my surprise, he had already had a feeling I was bisexual. Next, I will be telling my children. I would like to thank all involved for making *Call Me By Your Name*.

Anonymous
Los Angeles, CA
USA

I went to see *Call Me by Your Name* at the movies just by chance. Since it was up for an Oscar for Best Picture, I thought I would check it out. I never expected those 2 hours and 12 minutes to change my life. I had never seen a movie so beautifully made, as well as a movie that dominated my thoughts for days and weeks to come.

I immediately read the novel which was equally inspiring. Over the next several weeks, I went to see *Call Me by Your Name* twelve more times at the cinema (this from a person who had never watched the same movie in the cinema more than three times).

One way *Call Me by Your Name* has changed me is by inspiring me to become a more well-rounded individual. After seeing Elio constantly reading, listening to classical music, speaking different languages, playing the piano, knowing history, growing up around art, and being knowledgeable about so many topics, it made me realize just how little of my mind I use. I was envious of Elio. At such a young age, he was already a very bright, intelligent young man. Even though I always thought of myself as smart, here I was in my forties, and I realized just how little I knew. As a science and math teacher, I use my "left" brain constantly, but I have never really cultivated my "right" brain. That has changed since seeing *Call Me by Your Name.*

After watching the movie, I immediately started reading the books that were shown in the movie or mentioned in the novel. Edgar Allan Poe, Dante's *Inferno*, poetry by Antonia Pozzi, Stendhal's *Armance*, Pearl S. Buck's *Dragon Seed*, Marguerite de Navarre's *Heptameron,* Lucretius' *On the Nature of Things*, Joseph Conrad's *Heart of Darkness*, and Heraclitus – *The Cosmic Fragments* are just a few of the books. I felt if these books are good enough for Elio and Oliver, they should be a good start for me in my new adventure of reading.

I have never been a person to read much for pleasure. However, I have read more books in the last few months after seeing *Call Me by Your Name* than I have read in the last two decades of my life. I have also started listening to some classical music (of course, I started with Bach, Liszt, and Busoni!), and I even purchased a book about Monet's life and paintings. I even set a future goal to learn a new language (of course, I chose Italian), and I have added visiting Italy to my bucket list. As a teacher, I love how *Call Me by Your Name* seems to place a value on intelligence in such a subtle way. That is refreshing in this day and time.

Call Me by Your Name has also forever changed the way I view same-sex relationships. As a straight man, I always considered myself accepting of gay lifestyles, but I admit I never truly understood it. After seeing *Call Me by Your Name*, my viewpoint has forever changed. Truly, love is love. After seeing the love of Elio and Oliver develop between each other, it is now crystal clear to me that the love between two men or two women can be the same as the love that develops between a man and a woman. I think Elio's father sums it up the best, "How you live your life is your business."

I want to thank Timothée Chalamet, Armie Hammer, Luca Guadagnino, and André Aciman for forever changing my world viewpoint on love, as well as inspiring me to become a more well-balanced individual by opening up a world of literature, art, music, and language to me. Even though I wasn't expecting it, those 2 hours and 12 minutes have become a great investment on my living a more fulfilling life.

Jason S.
Nashville, TN
USA

This story that I would like to share is about my friend. I've already got his permission to share this.

So while I was watching *Call Me By Your Name* in our classroom, he suddenly joined in and started watching. After an hour, we finished watching it.

"I hope I find someone like Oliver." He started saying.

"Don't worry, you will." I said patting his back.

My friend is actually gay. And I support him with whatever he wants to do. One time he chatted with me, "I'm coming out."

"Coming out? Where?"

"My parents of course. I've tired of acting like a man in front of them."

"Oh. Well you sure about that?"

"Yeah. I'll inform you tomorrow or later."

Actually, I was the one who was more nervous than him. So I waited patiently for his response. A day passed and I'm worried about what happened.

Then the next day, on our school, in our classroom he told me great news.

His parents accepted him. At first his mom was disappointed, but then later on she accepted him. Not a son, but a daughter. (It's what he told me.)

"You know, because of *Call Me By Your Name*, I was able to conquer my fear."

Anonymous
Pasig City
Philippines

The film hooked me with its romantic content and very beautiful actors. I adore romantic films. I liked the ending of the film, because I was thinking that it was quite happy or happy enough – Oliver called Elio his name.

But my feelings totally changed after I had read the book. André Aciman is a master of involving the reader in the story 100 percent. Because of the intensity of the book, I totally got into it. I couldn't concentrate on my work. All my spare time was dedicated to the book and the love story which was condemned to fail.

The ending of the book broke me totally. I cried many days not exactly knowing why. Even watching Timothée Chalamet accepting his awards for his wonderful performance in *Call Me By Your Name* and listening his speeches thanking people, I cried like a child.

Suddenly, I shuffled everything I was living for and why. Because I have never felt such love for anybody, or maybe I haven't received such love from somebody. Maybe I'm seeking it, or maybe I'm desperate because I'm afraid I'll never experience such a strong, warm, careful, tender, real feeling from someone in whose arms I'd feel like a child who needs protection and unconditional love.

This film and incredible acting of Timmy reminded me that I also acted many years ago and I liked it, and I was good at doing it. So why haven't I even tried to do that professionally? So, this was the impulse to me to go to some castings. Maybe I'll succeed!

It's been a month of active reading, searching, watching, listening and sharing of "things that matter". The last time when I watched *Call Me By Your Name*, I was quite calm and didn't cry. So, I hope I'm recovering from my obsession and little by little I will back to my own life.

Whatever already happened or is going to, I'm glad I had and still have such an experience to feel something that never felt before.

This film has changed my opinion about the love between same-sex people. I wasn't strictly against gays or lesbians, but it looked a bit outside the norm to me. Watching this film, I understood that the main thing is love, and sometimes it occurs between two men as well as a man and a woman.

I think this is the most important thing, which turned out seeing the true love story revealed by great acting, directing, and producing. A masterpiece.

Ugne Jancyte
Vilnius
Lithuania

Prior to watching *Call Me By Your Name*, I had no idea that this beautiful film existed. It was late February, 2018 when I saw a live streaming mobile app promoting *Call Me By Your Name* in Facebook. I got curious and checked the comment section of the FB ad. I got really interested after seeing lots of good comments about the film and decided to download the online streaming mobile application. Though I immediately downloaded the app, I wasn't able to watch CMBYN after getting the app, due to my busy schedule. What I did was screen capture the FB ad about the film to make sure I would not forget the title.

It was already March when I remembered about the film and got the chance to watch *Call Me By Your Name*. It was after my birthday celebration. I was so drunk the night before and decided so stay at home the next day. I remembered the film and decided to watch it. Since I had a really bad hangover that day, I got sad after watching the film, but I fell asleep immediately.

The next day I woke up and walked straight to the bathroom to take a shower. While the cold water from the shower lingered on my skin, the story of the film hit me, and I got really emotional. The emotion, the characters, the story, and the scenes hit me so hard that I felt so sad. The hangover from the film was much stronger than the hangover I experienced from my birthday celebration.

When I got to work, I immediately checked CMBYN online and read as much as possible about the film and found out that the actor who played Oliver in the film was the same Armie Hammer who was in *Mirror Mirror, The Lone Ranger*, and *The Social Network*. Also the same day while researching the film, I got to be part of the *Call Me By Your Name Global Facebook Group* where I met a lot of great people.

This film reminded me of how beautiful and painful love can be. That it is a double-edged sword. That revealing your feelings to someone will always be hard to do and could either be the reason for you to be happy or put you in despair. Love is such a great feeling, but it could be the worst at times. However, the film made me realize that it always better to speak to free yourself from the uncertainty of love. The outcome will either make you or break you, but it is better than to suffer from the questions and assumptions of hiding what you truly feel.

The film also made me realize how important timing is when it comes to love. They say we need the perfect timing, but what if it already passed because of waiting? You create your tomorrow, and what you do today will build your tomorrow, so do it now and you will know it later. No perfect timing, just courage and acceptance.

Even today, I am still hooked on this beautiful film and did a lot of things I normally don't do. Since that shower moment where the film hit me so hard, I became a huge fan. I bought André Aciman's book and read it, even though I am not a big reader. I became a member of *CMBYN Philippines Messenger group chat* and met a lot of great people there. The group decided to meet, and it was the first time I met strangers who now became my friends because of the book.

Aside from the book I bought, it was the first time I bought a DVD. I bought a shirt that says, "Somewhere in Northern Italy" and will soon buy other shirts with phrases from the movie. Also, I encouraged my friends to watch the film, as I am really proud of it. Some of them felt the same feelings I had, but some of them didn't like it. I got really sad because they were not able to appreciate such a great film. But it is true that we cannot please everybody. Maybe they haven't experienced that kind of love yet, but surely they will.

I would like to express my happiness of being part of the *Call Me By Your Name Global Facebook Group*, as it opened a lot of opportunities to share a lot of things about the film. *Call Me By Your Name* is such beautifully written novel that turned into an amazing and heartbreaking film. I'm still watching the film and it's continuously making me feel love and heartbreak at the same time. I will never get tired of sharing how beautiful this film is.

John Nicolle Bueno
Marikina City
Philippines

On November 5th, 2017, three days after my 21st birthday, I watched the *Call Me By Your Name* at Taipei's Golden Horse Film Festival and it ignited the desire of every cell in me, for him.

His name is Jack, an office man in the company. He is everything a person could ever ask for on a man - tall, handsome, muscular, stylish, mature, decent, also difficult, arrogant, and 16 years older than me.

I am a part-time student in the office and he is the editor. At first, he was so aloof, just like Oliver. It seemed that he didn't even give a damn about my existence, always walking by without a glance or a greeting. So I worked hard just to get his attention, and I did. I never said no whenever he needed me, and I proved to him the ambition of being irreplaceable.

Gradually, I think he felt it. He began to chat with me, picking up any possible subject. I recognized every shirt of his, and he does, too, on me. We talked about the music of pop divas we share, though he seemed to be shy about his tastes.

He showed kindness in a possible decent way, and I want to give the same and more. I want to cross that line. I sunk, however, into a dilemma of reality. That's how we interact - nicety ornamented between every moment of indifference. I was in hell, maybe still am. My whole body craves him, and I do believe he knows it.

Whenever I made up my mind to give him up, he pulled me back to him like a loyal subject to his king. In such a relationship, I am Elio and he is Oliver. On my 21st birthday, he gave me the euphoria I had never had. A tiny greenhouse pot of mimosa was the coolest gift ever. A man of few words, he only reminded me to water it regularly, when I was awkwardly smiling ear to ear at him, fetching no appropriate words on the spot, either.

That's our thing, inside - life, desire, vitality, also worries and risks of tears, which all were encapsulated in his subtle, indifferent way of love. Days after, I sent a short clip to him of my finger tickling these shy tiny trees, in whose every leaf dwells my hope, desire, loyalty, and love for him.

Right after the screening of *Call Me by Your Name* on November 5th, when I stepped out of the theater, there were his messages. Again from a man with few words, he said, "Be careful. Don't kill it."

Be careful. Don't kill the friendship, the brotherhood, and possibly more? The movie and novel speak to my heart of this special relationship yet in the making. I am still Elio before the Piave Monument. I doubt if I have the courage to ever tell him how much I admire, worship, and crave him, my Oliver. However, after the movie, which I have since watched ten more times in theater and other media, I know for sure about the resolution of my heart, to be loyal, no matter what will come out, only to him, my love, my Oliver, my Jack.

"Be careful. Don't kill it."

"Right now, there's sorrow, pain. Don't kill it and with it the joy you've felt."

In response to Jack and Mr. Perlman, "I won't."

Ko-Hao Chang
Taipei
Taiwan

Italy. Colors. Warmth. It all comes to life and is breathtaking in *Call Me By Your Name*. It fascinates with every viewing. In whose world are we invited? Going away from the darkness of (ironically) day-to-day life, one can step in a place of the oneiric.

In the dark month of February, I could walk the streets of a never visited before Italy and sit on the benches of Elio's soul, swim in the eyes of Oliver. In the months of February and March, my depression rears its ugly head, but this year I've played a game of hide and seek with my demons. They've searched and searched, but I was in Moscazzano, marveling at a moving painting created by an artist named Guadagnino.

Luca Guadagnino. Sounds. Sun. Symbols. Frame after frame, a secret waltzes around. First in the form of a fish, then some lovers in the background, then a poetic repetition of knowledge – just like Ravel's *Une Barque sur L'Ocean*. They all scream: Come back! Come back to us. Let the piano lead… follow it.

Without a single tear shed, I watched time after time, letting Mr. Perlman's speech heal my soul. Without any hesitation, I went to Bergamo and Crema, learned Italian, spoke to locals who automatically became friends and called me "Tesoro", listened to a piano under the window of the Istituto Musicale, but more importantly, discovered Northern Italy.

I am going back, this time to Milano and Genoa. Am I seeing Italy with my own eyes or is my vision being clouded by Luca's? Call me by your name, beautiful country… because I love you as so many others have loved you before and many more will.

Thank you, Luca Guadagnino, for pointing out my soul's home. Thank you for sharing bits of yours. As Rimbaud said: "I followed him… I had to."

Lily Blackwood
Suceava
Romania

It all began with the book. I started it and couldn't put it down. And then I could not wait until the movie came out. I was there the first night it opened near me. I could not move when it ended. Tears rolled down my face and I could hardly breathe. From that moment, I knew I saw something that had affected me for life.

I went online and read and watched everything I could find about the movie, Timothée, Armie, Luca and André. I went back to see it five more times in the theater, bought the album and the audiobook. I couldn't wait until I could buy the movie.

I think a lot about it every day and try to figure out why this little film had this kind of impact on me. I have seen so many movies in my life, and have loved so many, but why has this one affected me as it has?

I think it is a perfect storm of so many things:

André Aciman's book and James Ivory's screenplay are where it all starts for me. The story is beautiful, and the source material is just amazing.

The love between Elio and Oliver is so pure and beautiful - two people connecting through their love of music, literature, and of course their physical attraction.

The acting is beyond perfection. The more I watch Timothée's Elio, I am astounded by the nuances and small little things he does with his eyes, mouth and whole body. The way he delivers his dialogue kills me. All of the actors are terrific - but Timothée is beyond belief.

The chemistry between Armie and Timothée is what makes Elio and Oliver so believable. I watched them in interviews as they toured the world together promoting the movie. It is so obvious that they really do love each other and loved making *Call Me By Your Name* together. Their love in the movie comes through so strong and is so sensual. When they kiss, you feel their love.

The way it was directed, filmed, all of the music - especially Sufjan Stevens's songs, are all so magical. And the Italian countryside - ahhh. So perfect.

The fact that love is allowed to grow and flourish without any judgement or harm is a joy to watch. Mr. Perlman's monologue at the end is probably the most moving and beautiful scene and it has stayed with me.

And I have to mention how impactful the last four minutes - watching Elio's face and how he goes from such sadness to an acceptance - that what he and Oliver had was real, true, and has changed him and will be with him forever.

I'm not sure I can completely explain why *Call Me By Your Name* has had such a strong impact. It's just a feeling that goes to my soul and to my core. I am so happy to have experienced this film, this feeling and to know I am not alone.

Binny Silverman
Riegelsville, PA
USA

I can fondly remember the first time I watched the *Call Me By Your Name* last December 28, 2017. Six months later and still, the memories are still as fresh as those peaches sprung up out of the tree. The happiness, the love, the pain and sadness still bite me every time I re-watch it or even just when I abruptly remember some scenes from the movie.

Call Me By Your Name reflects and saves my life today. --- Some 10 months ago, I was so depressed. My depression was situational, but it did become very physical and very emotional. It always does, if you live with it long enough. And I did. I had good times. It wasn't all negative. I had plenty of good times. But I was depressed.

For months at a time, all I wanted to do was sleep. When you're depressed, even if you're having an amazing day, it feels like there is an ominous cloud over you, a constant reminder that it will start raining again soon. The toughest part about being depressed was the fact that I didn't want to get better. At the time, I couldn't see that, but I was hurting really badly. Depression was sort of a release; there was no other way to deal with the tremendous amount of pain I felt. I knew from the very start the reason why I felt that way. It is because of my closeted self that really bothers me.

Yes, I am not out yet, though some of my friends knew it. I am still not out to my family and I still can't have that freedom that other people like me can feel. It's really hard at times because I can't fool myself that I am happy when I am really not, I was scared to open up my problem to my family and I was so hopeless.

But *Call Me By Your Name* gives me light and shows me so much hope. After I watch it, I gain so much strength and faith to hold on to my life, to continue living and to be true to myself. I don't want to be scared anymore. I don't want to hide my real self and fool everyone around me. At that very moment, I realized that there is so much more in life and all we have to do is to trust in ourselves and just continue to show love. Just like how Mr. and Mrs. Perlman, Marzia and their whole family accept and understand what Elio's going through, I am also trusting my purest self (with all my heart and soul) that my family will accept me for who I really am.

And at this moment in time, I can barely imagine how I can continue to live my life if I wasn't able to watch *Call Me By Your Name* back then. Maybe I was messed up, miserable and got eaten by the darkness of depression. But now, I am here, alive and contented. I am really thankful that I got to witness the beauty of this film: the characters, atmosphere, the vibe and the totality of it. Thank you for showing not only me, but millions of people the beauty of life. Thank you for inspiring us and giving us all the hope we need to continue living the life given to us. Thank you *Call Me By Your Name* for making me the best version of myself. I love you!

Ram Santos Carlos
Cavite
Philippines

This movie, and the story itself, has touched me in two different ways.

The first way is that the story very much reminds me of my own story. It reminds me of what happened to me one summer, ten years ago. I could never quite let go of that summer, and of that person. But after reading this book, and after meeting these characters, reading their story, watching their story, I somehow found closure to my own story. I found a way to end a ten-year chapter of my own life.

In another way, it has affected me in a completely different way. I have health issues, and they cause me to sometimes have to stay in bed for weeks at a time. It can get me into a very negative headspace. But after reading the book, and watching the movie, I simply fell in love with both.

The characters, the story, the setting. Quite simply everything about it. This movie, this story, it has given me something positive. A lot of movies have a lot of negativity in it, but this movie feels so beautiful, so light, so positive, even with that ending. It feels like a breath of fresh air. It feels like summer. It puts a smile on my face when I'm ill, because I listen to the soundtrack, and it reminds me of the movie.

Before this movie, I would get back into that negative headspace. This movie, this story, it has somehow brought some light and positivity to my life. And I will forever be grateful for these characters and for their story, both in book and movie.

Samantha
The Netherlands

Films are made to entertain, but some are also made to stay in the back of your mind, even after you leave the theater. One way or another, these films will change the way you interact with your life and maybe even change your perception of the world. As much as we love watching typical Hollywood fluff movies, there is something remarkable about movies that are extremely relatable and human that would make us say, "I've been there" and *Call Me By Your Name* is one of those films.

This film is about the blossoming of love and desire which most of us have been through. So in this way, Elio's emotional turmoil and reluctance at first seems all too familiar. When he decided to tell Oliver how he felt, it is too relatable because we all know that expressing your feelings to someone is not easy and you don't want to say what you actually mean. But like Elio, we were also hopeful at that point and that hope is one of the things that we latch onto to help us keep going even though we don't know how things will turn out.

Eventually, that all too familiar unfortunate moment came to Elio and we were all left heartbroken. Now we are at this point in the film where Elio, like us in that specific time of our lives, was wondering, "Why did I even try?" And it's at this moment that Mr. Perlman gives advice that we all needed to hear or wished that we had heard after going through the same experience as Elio.

His whole monologue was a masterpiece, but the line that struck me the most was when he said, "To make yourself feel nothing so as not to feel anything - what a waste!" because for me, truer words has never been said.

As human beings, our initial reaction to these kinds of tragic moments in our lives is to force ourselves to not feel anything, to avoid a world of pain, but this film tells us to experience love and not be afraid to get hurt because whether we like it or not, being vulnerable is important for a relationship to work.

In the last powerful scene where Elio was sitting in front of a crackling fire while Sufjan Stevens' *Visions of Gideon* was playing in the background, you feel a beautiful bittersweet feeling when you hear the lyrics, "I *have loved you for the last time, is it a video?"* because it emphasizes that Elio can relish the memory, but never truly experience it again. That is how it is with all of us as well.

And when his mother calls his name and he turns around, I felt that this scene is showing us that this is not the end for Elio and also for us. The fire represents the summer that he and Oliver spent together and Elio was staring at it, not wanting to let go, but when he turned around, it is a symbol of courage that he is finally ready to move on.

For me, it is a wonderful portrayal that sometimes when we fall in life, we should have the courage to stand up again and move on even if we can't immediately forget.

D. B. Salazar
Manila
Philippines

Never would I have thought that a film could change a life! But that's what *Call Me By Your Name* did to mine. I first discovered the novel by watching the marvelous movie that left me with a mix of feelings of sorrow and joy. So I started the book from where the movie ended because I was really keen to know if these two beautiful human beings ended up together. And then again, I was left with a melancholy and pain that never went away.

I couldn't understand the ending at first, because I was relating the story to me and how missing some opportunities can haunt us for the rest of our lives. Every time I watch the movie, I feel like I'm escaping my own world to a place where I'm surrounded by an amazing family and a true lover.

However, there was one different thing for me and perhaps that's what

made me watch this film. I'm a Muslim girl from a very religious family and as you know, homosexuality is forbidden in my religion. In fact, I was neither a homophobic, nor a supporter. I was in a position where I didn't care because it didn't concern me. When this movie made a huge splash, I was like "Okay, let's give it try and perceive how two people from the same gender fall in love".

What left me speechless is throughout the whole film, I didn't even pay attention to the genders, I was mesmerized by this captivating and charming love story, thanks to Timothée and Armie who portrayed this relationship so perfectly and didn't make it look bizarre. Also, I find that the Perlman Family played a big role in supporting their child's choices. They encouraged Elio to be who he truly is, as they didn't frighten him into being what he's not.

It also taught me that it's better to embrace our sadness and not try to ignore it, because it only will get bigger and won't help us get over it.

This isn't a simple film. It offers a rare opportunity to interpret two peo-ple's incredible journeys of falling in love and more importantly, it makes you forget about their sexuality. Each scene only enriches the other and bolsters this already soaring story of love, lust, and longing. IT IS A LIFETIME EXPERIENCE.

Finally, a huge thank you to "Sweet Tea" Timmy, Armie, Luca, André, Michael, Amira, Esther, Victoire, Vanda and to everyone who was in-volved in making this magnificent movie. We love you and we can't wait for a sequel to recover from the ache we still feel.

Hanaa KHOJ
Tangier
Morocco

I saw *Call Me By Your Name* for the first time in March 2018. I partici-pated in an AMC screening of all the Best Picture Nominees. I had never heard of the film. I went with a couple who have been attending the screenings for years. They told me that Armie Hammer was in the film and it took place in Italy.

It was scheduled for day 2 of the screenings. Many of the films were impressive this year, but *Call Me By Your Name* was the 7th film we watched. I walked out of the film speechless. I couldn't quite say how I felt about it, but it lingered with me through the last 2 films of the night. I went home and slept on it (this was a Saturday). I bought the book the following Tuesday and read it in 3 days. I ordered the movie that week and watched it again.

Looking back, I can say several things. This movie spoke directly to my heart. I needed this movie, this body of work, to hold and keep close. I listened to the music constantly. The movie broke my heart and brought me into darkness. But ultimately, it meant everything positive to me and brought to me an urgency to experience life and to fight my anxieties and depression.

I see myself, although I am 36, as Elio. A brokenhearted young boy, who loves so deeply. Every moment of curiosity, joy, sadness, love, seduction etc., I felt it. I felt alone and abandoned with Elio at the end. And then I felt his happiness (maybe), that at least he had experienced this love. I closed my eyes when Michael Stuhlbarg gave his monologue to Elio in his office. I imagined that he spoke to me.

Call Me By Your Name taught me about experiencing life. To feel life fully. To love completely. To share yourself with those you love and the world around you. Maybe even recklessly, because life without all the feelings, ultimately means nothing.

Everyone involved with this film put everything into it; it's palpable. The performances by each actor and actress are the best moments of acting I have ever seen.

I got a puppy at the end of March. His name is Elio. This movie will be part of me forever. It changed me and how I view the world. It made me a better person.

Cara J Cacciabaudo
Milford, CT
USA

I'm one of the luckiest fans of *Call Me By Your Name*, mostly because I'm Italian ... and this gave me the chance to do many things. But let's start at the beginning.

I read the book back in 2007 when it was published for the first time in Italy, and to be completely honest, I wasn't enthusiastic. I appreciated it, but did not really feel it.

I'm a cinema addict. Since I was a child, movies and books were my best friends. So, I knew Luca Guadagnino's work and I loved any movie he made. *I Am Love* really stunned me!

Then I followed all of his work and I became aware of the film *Call Me By Your Name* during Fall 2016, when the movie was already shot and it wasn't yet a big thing. I read on Facebook that the movie was about to be presented at the Sundance (January 2017) Film Festival. A day later, I saw on YouTube a Q&A from Sundance with the cast and then something happened. Hearing them talk about the project strangely affected me and I started to get anxious about it.

Then I read that a few days later the movie would be shown at the Berlin Film Festival, and I immediately checked how I could get there and see the movie. Unfortunately the plane ticket was too expensive, and I couldn't leave work even for two days. So I had to wait for the movie to come out in Italy on January 25th. I was so excited!

I saw it in the original language (unusual because big movies are always dubbed, and I don't like this) and immediately something was triggered inside me. I felt connected to the movie like never before. It was like the story was there on the screen only for me, to let me know something, to push me. I'm gay and have been out since I was quite young. But I'm not really pretty and never have been loved. Seeing these two wonderful creatures falling in love with each other was really special!

I became aware that the next Monday after the opening, the film would be presented in Crema and Luca, Armie and Timothée would be there, too. I immediately started to search for a ticket and I went to Crema all by myself by car. It took around three hours but it worth it; it was worth it very much!!!

When I got there it wasn't really crowded which surprised me, but made me happy because that assured me that I really had the chance to meet the cast easily ... And then they came in to my life, FOR REAL! But it was hard to get to them through the crowds of young girls (I think I was one of the very few guys there) and I was a little bit intimidated.

I went prepared. I made gifts for them, a rose petal in which I wrote the quote from the book about the poet Shelley "Cor Cordium" (that I got tattooed on the side of my finger). I really couldn't get close enough to them, but I saw Elizabeth Chambers in a corner. Nobody was talking to her, so I approached her, and I explained to her that I had these gifts for Armie, Timmy and Luca. I asked her to give these petals to them for me. Immediately she said "No", but she took me by the hand and helped me reach her husband she called him when she was close enough and then he turned and smiled at me. I shook his hand and said, "Very nice to meet you." and he replied, "Nice to meet you too." He literally folded himself on top of me because he is so tall and I'm quite short! After that, I took out the petal gifts, explaining how the movie was touching and beautiful and that I hoped that these petals would bring him and the others luck and happiness.

He thanked me and smiled at me. I melted and almost fainted. I wasn't ready to ask him for an autograph or a selfie. Speaking to him was a special gift enough actually!

Then I immediately started to get closer to Timmy. I reached him and when I was ready with my phone to take a selfie with him, a bodyguard took him away from me and I said quite loud "Oh nooooo !!!" Timmy turned to me and smiled at me and he said "Stay there. I will come back..." I thought "Oh my god ... where do you think I will go ...?"

Then, in few minutes he came back directly to me and we took two amazing selfies! I found Elizabeth behind me and I thanked her because without that little push, I wouldn't have met Armie. I kissed her because I

149

was so grateful. Later I developed a deep addiction for the film. I went to the cinema nine times in all to see *Call Me By Your Name*.

Last month, in a town close to where I live, I took a class with Walter Fasano who edited *Call Me By Your Name* and all of the Guadagnino's other movies. He is a great friend of Luca. Fasano was amazing, a great movie lover. He spoke to us about the making of *Call Me By Your Name*, how it was on the set, about all other projects with Luca, and a little bit about the new project *Suspiria* and CMBYN sequels.

Last week in Bologna I finally had the chance to meet and speak with Luca and I gave him a very special t-shirt with many mini Elios printed on it, one for each outfit he had in the movie in chronological order. I finally had the chance to reward him, in my own way, about the great feelings that I felt anytime I saw the movie.

Speaking to him, while he was writing me an autograph, I asked him if Armie gave him the petal that I made ... and Luca, really honestly answered that he didn't receive it ... ahhhh what happened ?!?!?

Today I became aware that Luca is coming to Bologna next week to present the restored version of Dario Argento's original *Suspiria*!!! And you can bet that I will be there in the front row to see his new project! You can bet also that I will give him a new rose petal!

Enrico Cardinali Ganzerli
Modena
Italy

What has *Call Me By Your Name* meant to me? I'm not even sure where to begin ...it's crazy how much this movie has changed my life! At 52, I had been broken by love more times than I could count. I never wanted to see or hear another story, or anecdote, let alone a "meet cute" about love if I could help it.

In 2008, when I was planning to come out to my oldest daughter, she gave me the book as a birthday present. I read it and LOVED it, but it didn't change me the way the movie did. There is something about the chemistry between Armie and Timmy that makes you believe in their love. I felt like I was watching a real relationship, not something fictitious, written by someone who didn't really know how it felt. I got to experience the actual beginning, when Elio began to feel like he was going to die without Oliver's touch, when Oliver realized that Elio was someone he had to have. Only Luca could give that to us, only Armie and Timmy.

The first time I saw the film I was shell-shocked ... the credits began to roll, and I wasn't sure how to feel... or what to feel. But I knew that feeling something was, without a doubt, a lame description. I couldn't breathe. Was this possible? Could you love like that? Could someone feel that way in real life? And it made me believe again ... made me think I could have that.

As a pansexual female, I never thought I would be affected by a movie about two men. But that's not what this was ... this was a story about two souls ...two souls that had found one another, even with all the ways they should have been kept apart, they still found their way.

And somehow, in the middle of this amazing movie, I found my true family...

I'd always been the weirdo, the black sheep if it's still appropriate to say that. My family just shook their heads when I spoke. I got the occasional "she was dropped on her head" story even, so it was hard to relate to anyone. I got married at 21 to hide my sexuality, and it damaged me, but I'm good, better even, than I was. Because of this film.

I found a community, people who felt as passionate, excited, emotionally connected to this film, like me! I knew I wasn't some crazy Stan who just wanted to have an interesting conversation with the stars...I felt connected. And I found love again, because of this film. A fellow "peach" who lives on the other side of the world... a best friend who lives in Sweden, who sometimes knows me better than I know myself. A young girl

151

in Alabama who is helping me heal my relationship with my oldest child by showing me how to heal my child and myself.

I have been given more than just a movie to adore, but a lifetime of family and friends. Thank you Armie, Timmy, Vanda, and especially Luca. This is so much more than a movie…

Melissa Goodwin
Del Rio, TX
USA

This movie and book destroyed me and saved me all at the same time. Every word, every note … is deeply anchored in my soul … Perfection in pure form! Maybe because I have loved exactly the same way… Maybe because I suffered in this way … Maybe because this love is still here, and this movie reminded me of it with a terrible power! But I could not imagine my life without this movie and this book! They reminded me of the girl I was, with my dreams and happiness…And because the words are powerless to describe what I feel … I stop here and… wish you SUCH love!!!

Kalina Ivanova Ivanova
Burgas
Bulgaria

Summer of 2016: I was visiting friends "Somewhere in Northern Italy." More specifically, Cerea. My days were filled with savory dishes and adventures in the countryside. My world seemed balanced and complete. Unbeknownst to me, just an hour east, principal photography began on *Call Me By Your Name*, a film that would in due time have a profound impact on me.

A year and a half later, a mysterious clip called "Play That Again" showed up in my Facebook feed. In it, Elio flirts with Oliver by playing a series of Bach variations on piano. It was done in a single take, which intensified the tension. Powerful. I immediately purchased a ticket at the Arclight Hollywood, one of only two theaters in Los Angeles showing the film.

I wasn't sure what drew me to the film. Maybe, like Elio, I too liked to read, play guitar and piano, and spoke multiple languages (including Italian and French). Or maybe it was because as a kid I spent a month with my family in Palermo and fell in love with the drowsy, romantic heat of an Italian summer. Or more likely, it was because I recalled the excitement and pain of falling in love for the first time and presenting my authentic self to that person. Whatever the reason, the movie was magical.

From *Hallelujah Junction*'s energetic rattling piano chords in the opening credits through the final teardrop during *Visions of Gideon* in the closing credits, I was fully entranced. I was lucky to attend several Q&A screenings with Luca Guadagnino, Timothée Chalamet and Armie Hammer. I was happy to get their autographs afterwards, but like everyone else, I was hungry to hear more stories about the making of this amazing film.

To date I have seen this film 35 times, something I have never done with any other film. This past May when I revisited my friends in Cerea, they surprised me with a fantastic road trip visiting almost all of the film locations in the movie.

Along the way I met many "peaches," who also came to Italy to retrace the steps of their favorite characters. Some even dressed up as Elio in striped shirts or as Oliver garbed in "Billowy."

All had fascinating stories of how the movie affected them, of how it gave them courage to come out, or how it changed their views on love. "Love is love is love," said Armie in one of our post-show discussions. Mr. Perlman's speech," he added, "changed the way I will raise my children." If more people were as equally enlightened, life on Earth would be peachier.

John James Hickey
Elizaville, NY
USA

I still remember the first time I saw this film. Of course I say first, because I have seen it many more times since. I remember feeling like my heart sank, mixed with butterflies and then I realized: this movie captured the essence of falling in love. In two short hours, it's as if I had experienced first love myself. I had fallen in love, been cheated on, had high hopes and then broken up all throughout the course of this film.

The scene that I most identified with and touched me the most was Elio's crying scene by the fire. The emotions running through Elio's face as tears rolled down his face paired with Sufjan's beautiful music were all too relatable. It is the movie I never knew I needed. This film is pure beauty, love and heartbreak.

Ricky Baeza
San Francisco, CA
US

Thinking about Oliver's decision to get married: that was totally predictable given the time period. Practically every bisexual man I met during the 1980s and 1990s invariably ended up in a heterosexual relationship-- because it was so much easier, because heterosexual privilege was so pronounced. In fact, I can't remember a single bisexual in those years who ended up in a same-sex relationship. Which was doubly ironic (and tragic), as practically all the "bisexual" men I met at that time actually preferred men. I assume Oliver was one of them, given his "coma" comment in the book.

As for Elio, I don't buy his bisexuality for a second. Nor did Marzia, who saw right through him from the beginning. She knew Elio was pursuing her sexually that night after dancing because Oliver had been kissing Chiara. She forgave Elio at the end of the film and offered her friendship

154

because she knew (though I do wonder if there was anything in that poem he gave her that disclosed what was going on with him). It seems pretty clear that the Elio in the novel pursues only men after Oliver-- and Chalamet plays Elio to that effect. I forget which review pointed this out, but his body language when he's with Oliver is completely different from when he's with Marzia. With Marzia, he's more playful and in command (as if playing a role, perhaps?); with Oliver, he completely collapses as if under a spell.

And, I have to say, that the number one reason this film hit me so hard (despite its lack of development) was Timothée Chalamet's performance. To call it masterful would be an understatement. This guy is an absolute natural. His unspoken gestures throughout the film simply gutted me.

Everyone credits Michael Stuhlbarg's powerful monologue at the end of the film, and rightly so. But I'm sure all of you who have watched the film multiple times noticed that the scene works so powerfully not only because of Stuhlbarg's great rendition of Aciman's words, but also because of the cutaways to Chalamet. His face in that scene, his ever-so-subtle shaking his head no when his father asked if he was speaking out of turn, his moving toward his father the way he did when he said that Oliver was better than he is-- all of it broke my heart. But, then again, he shattered me probably 30+ times throughout the movie. God, I can't wait to see him in "Beautiful Boy."

Anonymous
Los Angeles, CA
USA

🖤🖤🖤🖤

Call Me By Your Name is not merely an obsession with a movie. It is not just a "film experience". It is like a portal. A key to a door within ourselves that flings wide open and gives ourselves back to ourselves.

It's not that it has given us something we didn't already have, per se, but that it unveils that which we already have within us, that has been locked away or denied for far too long, finally allowing us to reconnect to our inner joy and bliss again.

Anonymous

Is it better to speak or to die ?

To M *"If there is any truth in the world, it lies when I'm with you, and if I find the courage to speak my truth to you one day ..."* This piece, dedicated to you, is 'it', as close as I will ever get. (I therefore hope by some miracle, its destiny is to find its way to you).

"It is still alive for me, still resounds with something totally present, as though a heart stolen from a tale by Poe, still throbbed under the ancient slate pavement to remind me that, here, I had finally encountered the life that was right for me but had failed to have."

We were late for the airport, I feigned to JP, M's father that I'd forgotten something and ran back into the house, up the stairs, through the windy loft, creaking loose floorboards beneath my feet, to M's rooftop room, he looked grief-stricken, startled he was relieved to see me again. We kissed passionately for the last time, cheeks moist as tears streamed from our eyes. My world was crumbling.

"I suddenly realized that we were on borrowed time, that time is always borrowed, and that the lending agency exacts its premium precisely when we are least prepared to pay and need to borrow more..."

Before returning to the car where JP was waiting, puzzled and impatient, unaware of the events of the last six weeks that had unraveled that summer, somewhere in South-West France, a surrogate paternal figure to me for the past decade, he looked perplexed at my apparent visible, disproportionate, distress, I tried hard to mask the pain and fight back the tears on the journey to the airport, where I was headed overseas to begin university.

"Let summer never end, let him never go away, let the music on perpetual replay play forever, I'm asking for very little, and I swear I'll ask for nothing more."

"Everyone goes through a period of Traviamento - when we take, say, a different turn in life, the other via. Dante himself did. Some recover, some pretend to recover, some never come back, some chicken out before even starting, and some, for fear of taking any turns, find themselves leading the wrong life all life long."

And so it is that unbeknownst to me, all along, I have been pretending to recover and perhaps even, living the wrong life.

That day my heart shattered into a thousand pieces, it broke, and had never fully mended. Until by Grace, I stumbled upon *Call Me By Your Name*.

A year or so later, with distance and time, M announced to me on the phone that he was with someone, F. During my time overseas at university they married and eventually had children together. ***"We belonged to each other, but had lived so far apart that we belonged to others now."***

"He came. He left. Nothing else had changed. I had not changed. The world hadn't changed. Yet nothing would be the same. All that remains is dream-making and strange remembrance."

We have never officially broken up. I had relationships, none as pure and wholesome as M. I never married nor had children, then eventually became so ill that to this day, I am mostly housebound or bed-bound. So there will never be the opportunity to see my 'M' again, if not but to hold him tight and tell him that I love him in a way I never knew I could love anybody else.

"Part of it— just part of it —was a coma, but I prefer to call it a parallel life. It sounds better. Problem is that most of us have— live, that is— more than two parallel lives."

My life with M is happening somewhere in a parallel universe. If I knew then what I know now, I would never have followed the call of duty and left for university. Instead I would have stayed, for everything I ever cherished was right there - M, the country house, his parents JP & F, sisters M & J, the lake, the garden, the pool, the plum trees.

"They can never undo it, never unwrite it, never unlive it, or relive it- it's just stuck there like a vision of fireflies on a summer field toward evening that keeps saying, You could have had this instead."

Safe in his arms and through the windows of his eyes, the soothing sound of his heart beating against my temple, whispers in the twilight, silence as we lay in the grass staring up at the blue sky and fluffy clouds. *"If I could have him like this in my dreams every night of my life, I'd stake my entire life on dreams and be done with the rest. "*

In this entire universe he still feels like "home" to me.

"You are the only person I'd like to say goodbye to when I die, because only then will this thing I call my life make any sense."

I have thought of writing to M many times. I even tried to move back to that region of the South-West of France believing it would heal my body, likely broken from a broken heart that never mended. That I could stay at the house with his parents JP and F. Search and find the pieces that would patch me up again. As though the house would recognize me, welcome me home and heal me. The cooing of the mourning doves, their lullaby, soothing my restless heart. For if I'm honest, I've spent my whole life secretly attempting to return. Even now, like a compass guiding me home. I can hear the village bells ringing, calling him by my name, and I by his.

I did reunite with JP & F (his parents) briefly in a nearby village a few years ago and the joy and love between us remained abundant. Despite the years, it was as though not a moment had passed - *"Twenty years was yesterday, and yesterday was just earlier this morning, and morning seemed light-years away."*

It felt like just yesterday that we were "being called for dinner" where we had breakfast and dined alfresco together between swims at the lake in our 80s espadrilles, swimming trunks, friendship bracelets and colourful bathing suits. Picking Mirabelle plums from the trees. Our fondness and love for each other not a day old. Not knowing whether M was still married, I didn't have the courage to ask. JP & M were, I noted, deliberately ambiguous. I sensed M may have been separated trying to work things out but I cannot know for sure. With illness I lost the courage "to speak", and I, like Elio in the book, who did not want to go meet Oliver's wife and children, did not want to hamper my memories, nor disturb anyone's life. So I held my tongue and, possibly, died all over again.

"Was it that I was jealous of his family, of the life he'd made for himself, of the things I never shared and couldn't possibly have known about? Things he had longed for, loved, and lost, and whose loss had crushed him, but whose presence in his life, when he had them, I wasn't there to witness and wouldn't know the first thing about. I wasn't there when he'd acquired them, wasn't there when he'd given them up."

"Over the years I'd lodged him in the permanent past, my pluperfect lover, put him on ice, stuffed him with memories and mothballs like a hunted ornament confabulating with the ghost of all my evenings. I'd dust him off from time to time and then put him back on the mantelpiece. He no longer belonged to earth or to life. All I was likely to discover at this point wasn't just how distant were the paths we'd taken, it was the measure of loss that was going to strike me--a loss I didn't mind thinking about in abstract terms, but which would hurt when stared at in the face, the way nostalgia hurts long after we've stopped thinking of things we lost and may never have cared for."

"This is where I dreamed of you before you came into my life."

M and I grew up together I was 8 when I first set eyes on him, M (with two Ts), my best friend from primary school's older brother. I was mesmerized, and immediately sensed we would belong to each other someday. During our teenage years there was magnetism and tension between us. I didn't know if he noticed me and sometimes it felt as though he kept his distance and ignored me.

"I always tried to keep him within my field of vision. I never let him drift away from me except when he wasn't with me. And when he wasn't with me, I didn't much care what he did so long as he remained the exact same person with others as he was with me. Don't let him be someone else when he's away. Don't let him be someone I've never seen before. Don't let him have a life other than the life I know he has with us, with me. Don't let me lose him. I knew I had no hold on him, nothing to offer, nothing to lure him by. I was nothing. Just a kid."

As the years went by there was an intense inexplicable push and pull between us, much like Elio and Oliver - moments I waited and longed for him, tensions between us. We spoke, we didn't speak, we explored with stolen touches sometimes in the pool or at the river other times at night and during the day curious, innocent moments. We couldn't control the emotions and magnetism that drew us together.

"Did I want him to act? Or would I prefer a lifetime of longing provided we both kept this little Ping-Pong game going: not knowing, not-not-knowing, not-not-not-knowing? Just be quiet, say nothing, and if you can't say "yes," don't say "no," say "later." Is this why people say "maybe" when they mean "yes," but hope you'll think it's "no" when all they really mean is, Please, just ask me once more, and once more after that?"

One evening past midnight finally circumstances brought us together. Overwhelmed by my feelings for him, under the bedcovers, I panicked and scampered out of the room.

"I craved him, but I could just as easily live without him, and either way was fine. I was happy, and this was all that mattered, with others, without others, I was happy."

The following day we went back to our awkward silences, snatched glances and the unbearable longing. Bewildered, I could not comprehend my reaction, explain it, not even to myself.

It wasn't till a year or so later when I came to stay at the C's family home for six weeks over the summer break age 18, he aged 21 that finally, after all those years, 10 years, the stars aligned.

"Perhaps we were friends first and lovers second. But then perhaps this is what lovers are."

M kissed me, passionately, in the garden one night after dinner, under the stars and from then on we fell deep. ***We had the stars, you and I. And this is given once only.*** I would sneak through the creaking windy loft to his room every night "You call me by your name and I'll call you by mine". We talked and made love till the early hours when I'd have to sneak back to my section of the loft early morning, before his parents awoke.

"It would finally dawn on us both that he was more me than I had ever been myself, because when he became me and I became him in bed so many years ago, he was and would forever remain, long after every forked road in life had done its work, my brother, my friend, my father, my son, my husband, my lover, myself."

"From this moment on, I thought, from this moment on—I had, as I'd never before in my life, the distinct feeling of arriving somewhere very dear, of wanting this forever, of being me, me, me, me, and no one else, just me, of finding in each shiver that ran down my arms something totally alien and yet by no means unfamiliar, as if all this had been part of me all of my life and I'd misplaced it and he had helped me find it. The dream had been right—this was like coming home"

JP and F who had been loving and kind surrogate parents & Family to me for many years, knew nothing of the love blooming between us, althhough at dinner al fresco in the evenings his mother kept pointing out something was different about her sweet boy, until one evening while running her fingers through his hair, she blurted out "I know what it is sweetheart, you're in love!". I almost choked. I had to keep a straight face so as not to give away with whom, but my heart was overwhelmed with joy as I knew this was the greatest confirmation to me, F was my Annella. A mother knows, and she saw in him, his feelings of deep love (for me)."Parce que c'était lui: parce que c'était moi" - Montaigne. JP & F did not find out we were together, that it was me he was in love with, until I was long gone (or so they led us to believe).

And gone I was. And gone I have been. From my true life. The parallel life. Where love reigned and everything that ever felt true to me was. Like home.

"This was the best person I'd ever known in my life. I had chosen him well." His parents were my parents, his sister my best friend and he the husband I believed he would be in my age 8 innocence as I gazed at this beautiful 11-year-old creature and in that childlike purity knew in my heart that this was the love of my life. I was right. My love grew for 10 years and never ended. It remains today. Although he may never know it.

And I've kept this secret for 24 yrs.

"Time makes us sentimental. Perhaps, in the end, it is because of time that we suffer."

To you M "Cor cordium, heart of hearts, I've never said anything truer in my life to anyone."

Anonymous

Bold Italics – Aciman, André . 2007 *Call Me By Your Name*. New York, N. Y.: Farrar, Straus, and Giroux

Has *Call Me By Your Name* touched you or changed your life?

To be included in volume 2, write us at cmbynbook@gmail.com.

If you want to join the international CMBYN Facebook group:
https://www.facebook.com/groups/CMBYNglobal

To join the Call Me By Your Name Fan Support Twitter group:

https://twitter.com/CMBYNFanSupport

Profits from the paperback book go to The Trevor Project.

About The **Trevor Project**

The Trevor Project is the leading and only accredited national organization providing crisis intervention and suicide prevention services to lesbian, gay, bisexual, transgender, queer, and questioning (LGBTQ) young people. The Trevor Project offers a suite of crisis intervention and suicide prevention programs, including TrevorLifeline, TrevorText, and TrevorChat as well as a peer-to-peer social network support for LGBTQ young people under the age of 25, TrevorSpace. Trevor also offers an education program with resources for youth-serving adults and organizations, a legislative advocacy department fighting for pro-LGBTQ legislation and against anti-LGBTQ rhetoric/policy positions, and conducts research to discover the most effective means to help young LGBTQ people in crisis and end suicide. If you or someone you know is feeling hopeless or suicidal, our Trevor Lifeline crisis counselors are available 24/7/365 at 866.488.7386.

www.TheTrevorProject.org

164

Made in the USA
Lexington, KY
09 December 2019